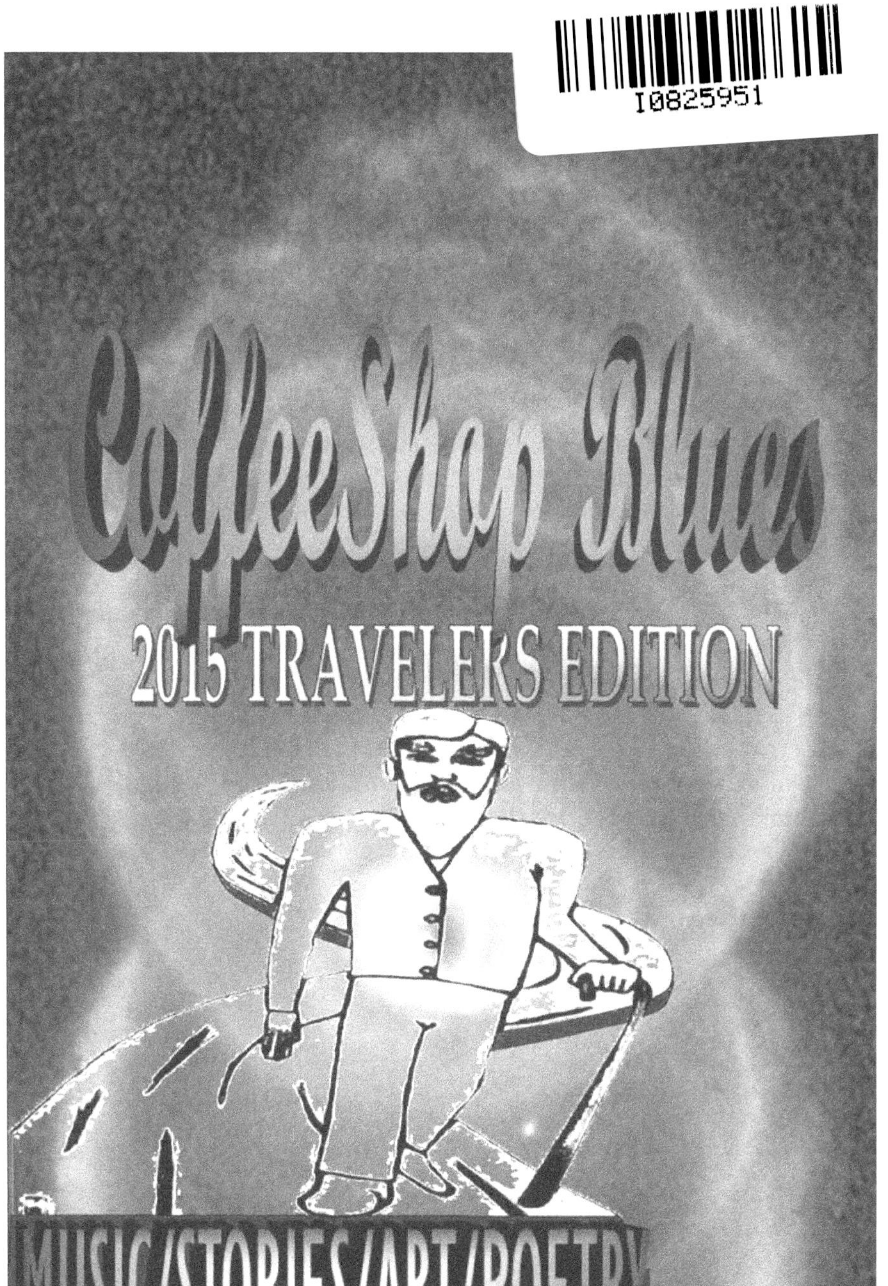
CoffeeShop Blues
2015 TRAVELERS EDITION
MUSIC/STORIES/ART/POETRY

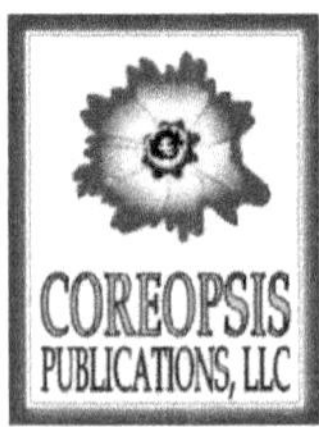






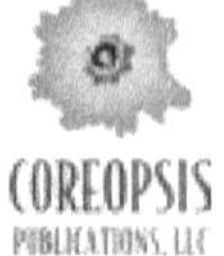


Coreopsis Publications, LLC
P. O. Box 5869
Titusville, Florida 32783



ISBN-13:
978-0-9763029-5-7

ISBN-10:
0-9763029-5-0

Library of Congress Control Number: 2015903474

# CoffeeShop Blues

## TRAVELERS EDITION

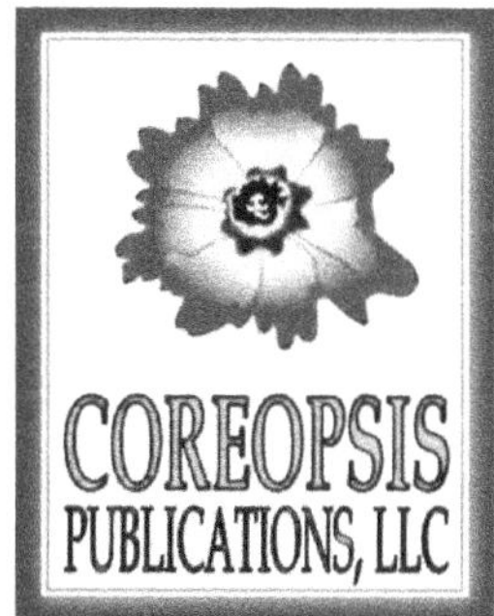


P. O. Box 5869
Titusville, Florida 32783
**www.Coreopsis.gs**
Coreopsispress@gmail.com

# TABLE OF CONTENTS

COUNTRY MUSIC NEWS INTERNATIONAL

# Letter from the Editor

This has, so far, been one of the most challenging projects I have undertaken. Sure, I've been making books for a long time, and it was my job while I was in Taiwan. Also, I have extensive editing experience in all sorts of genres. But, trying to preserve the writer's voice, tone, mood, and culture can be extremely difficult when crossing continents.

If not for my experience overseas I may have never realized how many different forms of the English language there truly are. In this edition there are words and phrases that, to you, may seem like spelling errors (trust me, I thought there was one myself), but that just goes to demonstrate what I am writing about.

This time I thought it would be a bit easier, but wound up all in my lap again. I really only know of a couple of others that I would have trusted it to anyway. The writers, poets, artists, and musicians really stood patiently by and they all deserve enormous amounts of praise for their work. By purchasing a copy from them you are supporting their continuation of work in the arts. The links to their work are all in place so even each reader of even the digital copies can find them, like them, follow them, purchase their work and help support them in their passions.

This really couldn't have been completed without the help of a few others that I should mention. I really have to thank public domain for a great deal of help with this. I want to thank the Hubble Telescope for supplying the picture for the background cover photo. I'd also like to thank the CIA and their wonderful mapmakers. Nathaniel Schellhase Hvisdos has been there from the beginning and has been a real driving force behind this. Also, Country Music News International, who I write music reviews for, is how I wind up meeting so many of these bands. That's how I came across Milagro Saints. From that first review I wound up in contact with Stephen David Ineson, who has been incredibly helpful with providing me with the new album cover, background, interview, and some of the first tracks to be released. Michael Christopher Markman has been there from the beginning as well.

I really hope that if you are reading this you take the time to follow the links of the people whose work rests within these pages.

It's kind of hard to produce these without any advertisers and I am not too good at blindly approaching them. If anyone out there knows of any respectable international companies or ones that need international exposure and would like to support our cause don't hesitate to contact us. I hope that we can keep producing these journals and many more issues will follow. All across this Earth, there are a lot of great writers/artists/poets/and musicians that just need an avenue to get their work out.

Thank You,

Jeremy Frost
**Coreopsispress@gmail.com**

# INDIA

India
International boundary
State or union territory boundary
National capital
State or union territory capital
Expressway
Road
Railroad
AFGHANISTAN
Kabul
Islamabad
PAKISTAN
CHINA
NEPAL
Kathmandu
Thimphu
BANGLADESH
Dhaka
BURMA
Rangoon
New Delhi
Delhi
Jaipur
Jodhpur
Agra
Lucknow
Kanpur
Patna
Bhopal
Jabalpur
Indore
Ranchi
Kolkata
Nagpur
Raipur
Cuttack
Bhubaneswar
Mumbai
(Bombay)
Pune
Hyderabad
Vishakhapatnam
Kakinada
Vijayawada
Chennai
(Madras)
Bangalore
Pondicherry
Mangalore
Calicut
Cochin
Madurai
Trivandrum
Kavaratti
SRI
LANKA
Colombo
Galle
Trincomalee
Arabian
Sea
Bay
of
Bengal
Andaman
Sea
ANDAMAN
ISLANDS
Port Blair
NICOBAR
ISLANDS
INDIAN OCEAN
MALDIVES
INDONESIA
Boundary representation is
not necessarily authoritative

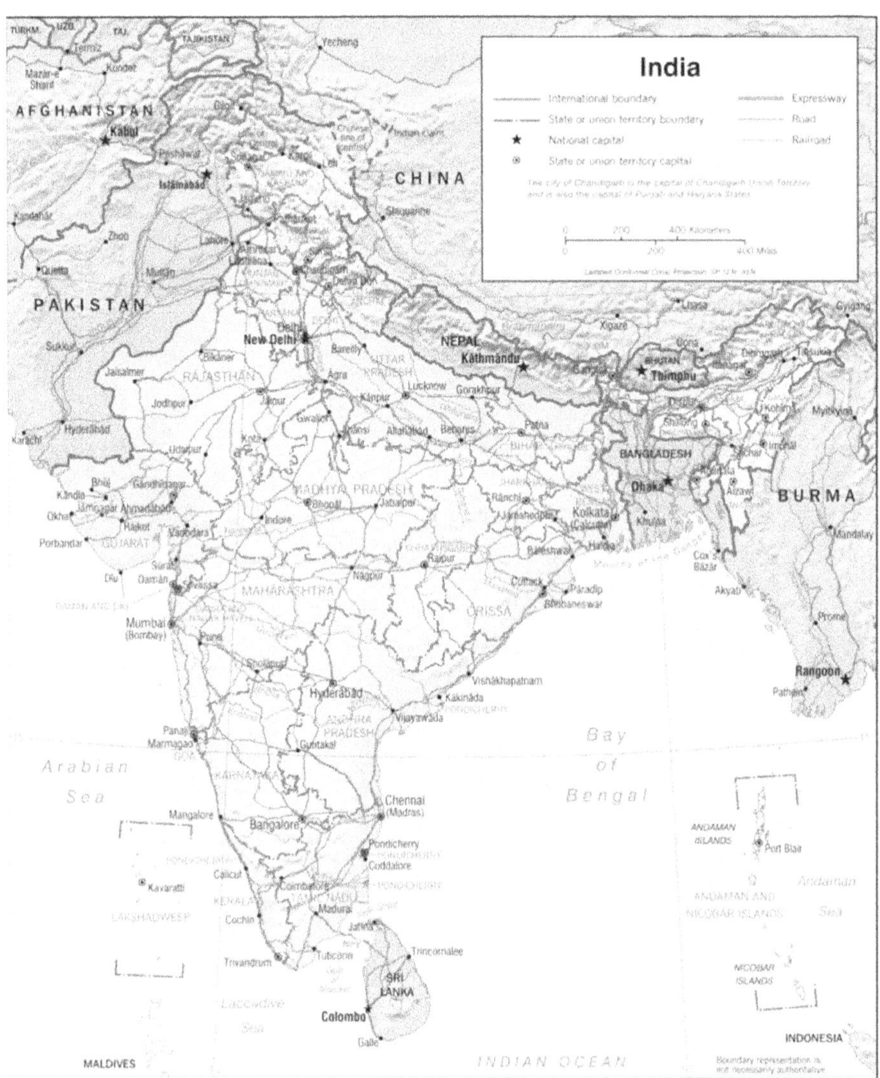

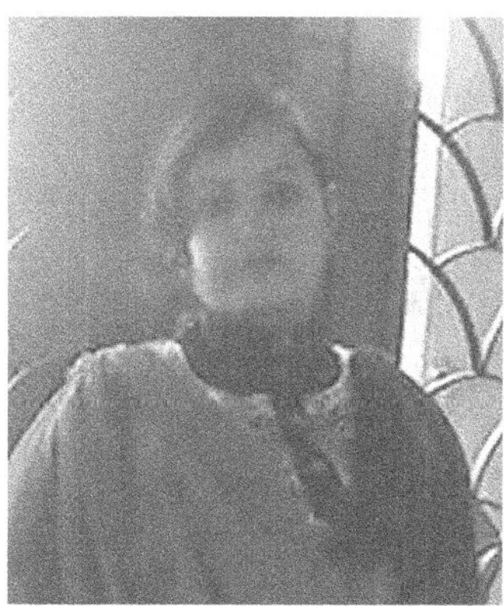

# Koyel Mitra

Koyel Mitra has a Masters in Mathematics and currently pursuing Bachelor in Education. She is the author of 6 books-3 poetry and 3 short stories so far. She teaches Math at a high school. She has an upcoming 7th book. All my books can be found at my website **www.koyelevergreen.wordpress.com**

# That Inevitable Truth

(A True Ghost Story)

I was about the age of twelve when I had taken a trip to Delhi along with my parents. My father had a boyhood friend named Mr. Roy who had a grand mansion-like apartment in Delhi we used to stay at.

As far as I recollect, the city was really beautiful. The capital of India, nearly fifteen years before, was far more posh, clean and ultramodern than contemporary Kolkata, where I resided.

I visited almost all of the ornate, pristine monuments of Delhi like the Qutub Minar, Red Fort, and the other citadels created by the ancient rulers of India. Those places of extreme historical importance seemed to enchant me. I began to form a strong penchant for this place.

The first day at that magnificent apartment turned out quite drab. After our return from the tourist spots on the second day my head began to reel and fatigue almost numbed my arms and legs. With blinking eyes and deep sleep fishing in my eyelids, I almost gobbled my dinner and jumped onto my bed. My room was adjacent to that of my parents.

I curled myself in cozily on the white pillows and matching bedspread, and fell fast asleep. A sudden gust of chilly wind from the open window rattled my spine and I sat up bewildered, staring blankly at the curtains; swishing to and fro. It was early November and the weather was pleasant. I wondered about the sudden cold wind this early in the season. I mused on the whereabouts of the cold breeze but finding no clue fell asleep.

The amber sunlight perforated through the glass windows and swept over my eyes. I woke up bleary. After brushing my teeth and having my breakfast, I again went out to rummage the centers of attraction and spotted a number of forts. It was the third day and as usual after my routine dinner my muscles began to ache, and I fell asleep.

The abrupt whines of a child startled me. The mysterious cry formed goose bumps on my skin. With quaking hands, I lit the candle on the table next to my bed. It was exactly twelve o'clock. Several beads of perspiration began to form on my forehead. And, an unknown fear paralyzed me.

I cried in panic, "Please help. Help! "

My parents scurried from the next room. "What's the matter dear? Why are you screaming like this? Is anything wrong?"

I told my parents about the events over the past couple of days. They furrowed their eyes and exchanged their glances.

My dad said, "My little girl, be steady. We cannot hear any outcry as you have described to us. It must be your crazy whim. Be courageous, my darling."

"Dad, believe me. Please believe me. It is not any illusion or caprice. It is an austere truth. This house is haunted." My dad embraced me with both his hands.

My mother said, "Everything is going to be fine sweetie. Stop reading ghost stories for now and clear your mind of those things. Good night. Sleep tight."She placed her tender hands on my head and they went away. I heaved a sigh of relief and soon fell asleep.

The tangerine sun splintered the glass and its lurid glare at me shook me up from the bed. It was the fourth day and according to our schedule, we had completed our routine itinerary. After gulping down my dinner, I stomped into my bed and fell asleep.

The clinking of the wind chimes perplexed me, so I lit the candle and squinted to see the clock. Once again it was exactly twelve o'clock. A chill swept down my whole body and almost shook my bones. I tried not to disturb my parents.

By this time I had a hunch that this house was spooky, and there was some evil spirit lurking inside it. It also came into my mind that this spirit for some reason or the other had decided to visit me, make me its victim and had not chosen my parents.

I murmured the name, Holy Lord, and with the dim light of the candle, goggled outside my window. I took a glimpse of the ebony velvet with twinkling stars interspaced in between.

The low whines of a child again started. I began to chant the name of The Almighty and peered into the black canopy. A pale face of a child fished out of nowhere and formed shudders throughout my whole body.

With utmost fortitude, I mumbled, "Who is it?"
There was no answer. I repeated the question louder.

A toddler with a small, frail figure climbed out of the window and waddled in front of my bed. I began to swoon and stutter.

"Who –a-r-e y-o-u?"

"Don't fear Koyel." The boy resonated with confidence.

With a dry throat I whispered, "How come you know my name?"

The boy smirked and grinned. "Spirits are undead. They know everything, even about the things beyond this Earth. They can foretell. The only trouble is the deep, burning angst in their hearts."

With squinted eyes I almost choked, "What is it that you have got to tell me?"

"Do you want to listen? Will you really punish that grisly crime?"

With this, the boy shouted and flailed his arms wildly.

With blood curdling in my heart and taking deep breaths, I said, "Okay. Go on boy."

"My name is Hari. I am the unborn son of the first wife of your uncle Mr. Roy, who murdered my mother hideously."

I gasped and could not utter any single word.

Hari went on, "My mother Meera was an educated woman and the only daughter of a wealthy zamindar. Your uncle promised to marry my mother after having a furtive affair of three years. My innocent mother yielded herself completely to her first love, body and soul.

The poor girl got pregnant and she broke this unpleasant news to your uncle. Your uncle ordered her to have an abortion. My guileless and compassionate mother revolted that, and so your uncle killed my mother with his ruthless, vile hands to efface that inevitable offence, and buried her, here, in the groves.

Your uncle then broke her cupboard and ransacked all the cash and expensive jewelry out of there and fled to Kolkata. Mr. Roy is a reputed businessman there and happy with his second wife and two children but what about this hideous crime? "

The face of Hari glowered and his maw dropped. He began to fidget in a frenzy of unbridled rage.

I stood dumb-struck at this extremely quaint reality. I was shell-shocked by this absolute truth. The face of my uncle flashed for a second, and my blood froze when I realized him to be a deadly criminal.

With quivering lips I said," Yes, I agree with you but what can I do for you Hari?"

"Just jail him. I know your dad is a deft lawyer and he will be able to execute this."

I said, "Okay. I will. Will that put your soul to rest?"

"Of course!" Hari bellowed. "I want peace."

"I agree with you Hari." The figure disappeared.

The morning sun painted the sky with vivid, vibrant hues of rosy-pink. I got bemused by the exquisite beauty of Mother Nature. It was five o'clock in the morning. The birds started chirping and fleeting across the sky. For about two hours I ruminated on the previous night's happening and finally reported that to my parents.

My parents got confounded, and began to stammer at this sheer incredible but inevitable truth.

On our return to Kolkata my dad enquired about Mr. Roy, and got the required information through his secret clientele. Mr. Roy was given a life-time imprisonment for his heinous crime. I never had a nightmare after that, and even today when I sleep alone nothing appears at midnight.

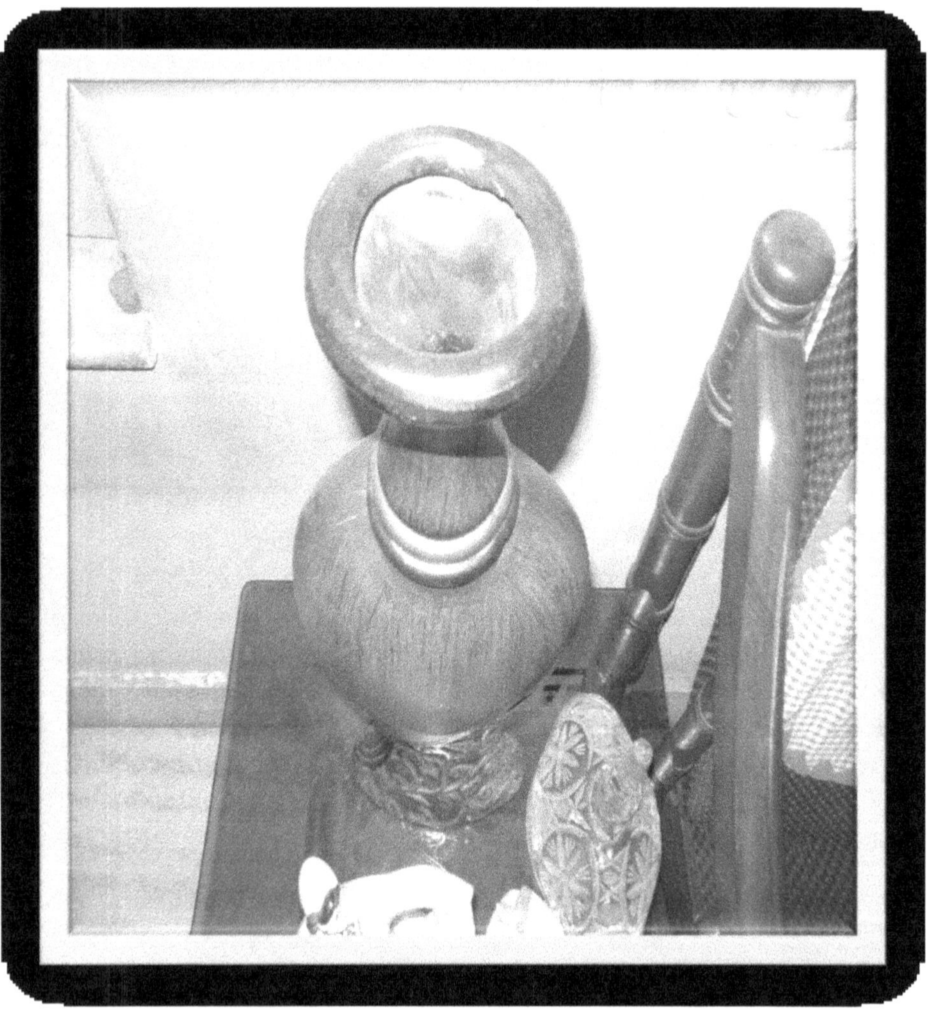

# GERMANY

DEN.
North Sea
Baltic Sea
Neuendorfer bei Wilster
Kiel
Rostock
Lübeck
Bremerhaven
Hamburg
Emden
Bremen
BERLIN
POL.
Hannover
NETH.
Magdeburg
Duisburg
Essen
Leipzig
Düsseldorf
Kassel
Dresden
Cologne
Bonn
BEL.
Frankfurt am Main
Wiesbaden
CZECH REPUBLIC
Rhine
Mannheim
LUX.
Nürnberg
Karlsruhe
Stuttgart
Danube
FRANCE
Munich
AUSTRIA
Zugspitze
0 50 100 km
0 50 100 mi
SWITZ.
LIECH.

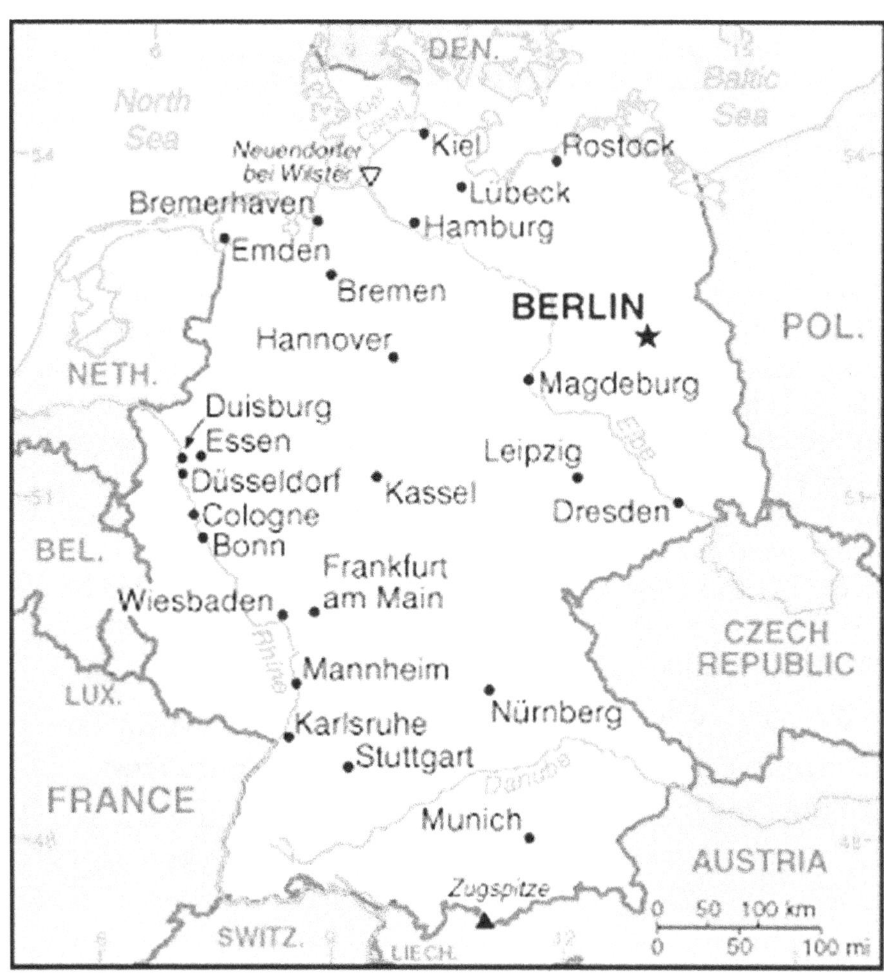

# KENNETH SCHROEDER

Kenneth Schroeder is currently writing about the walk he made from Portugal to the Middle East, and he may be writing about it for a long time as it has taken one whole year to write about a four-month period of the 18-month walk. Ken lived in Portugal for 15 years before a religious experience on a mountain set him in motion to make peace in the Middle East. After leaving a trail of war and revolution in his wake, Ken returned to Europe, flying in to Milan from Egypt, and bought a cheap bike for a new mission. He now lives in Germany, where he gave up on his cycling expedition to Syria after realizing he had gone 2000 kilometers in the wrong direction from Italy.

**Amazon.com: Poor Knights: A Trek through the Balkans (Down to Egypt Book 1) eBook: Kenneth Schroeder: Kindle Store**

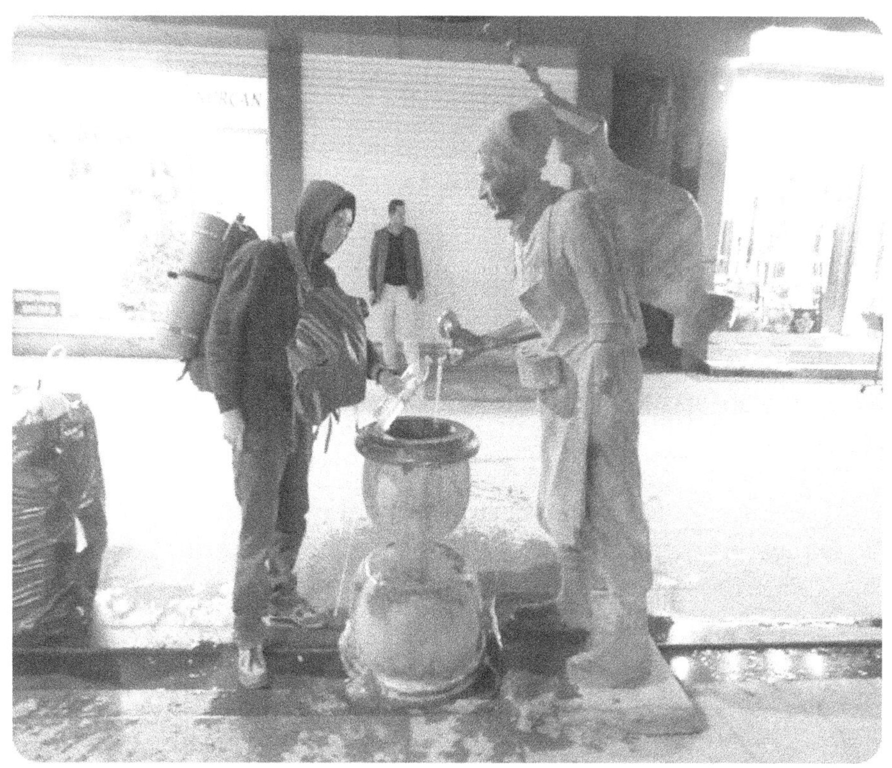

# Breaking into Schools

By:

**Kenneth Schroeder**

The sun is low, and it is time to camp, but there is no cover. At the edge of the village there is a school that is undergoing renovation. It is a one storey rectangular building, pink except for where the paint has flaked off. The school grounds are a bit overgrown, and rubbish is scattered near the school building. A flag pole leans near the entrance.

In silence Inge walks her bike down a side road to have a better look. I trudge behind her.

"Maybe we can sleep in here," she says.

The alternative is to pitch the tent out in the open near the village, where we will be seen. Also, it is cold, and it might rain again.

"Maybe so," I say.

There is a trailer parked near the school building—the construction contractor's office, perhaps. The light is already on in the trailer, though there are no workers anywhere.

We peer inside the school through a window that is ajar. We take turns scanning a storage room that is full of desks and chalkboards and lighting fixtures and construction material and dust. I push the window open a bit more—its frame is gray wood and the white paint on it has mostly flaked off. The wood is swollen so it is difficult to force it open but I manage to do it. I dump my backpack, the surplus army pack, and I lean my walking stick against the wall. I have a quick look around to see if anyone is watching, and I pull myself through the window and into the school.

"Wait," I say, brushing myself off. I spend a few minutes poking around the dusty rooms and there is a small pink room with mattresses in it, and I wonder for a moment why mattresses are in a school, but mostly I take it as a blessing to have the mattresses for us to sleep on. They are clean and dry.

"Okay," I say when I'm back at the window. "We can sleep here if we can find a way to get Suzy in."

"I come in too," Inge says, and she jumps a little and pulls herself through the window.

The double doors at the front are bolted, and a vertical metal bar fastens them to the floor, but I slide the metal bar up and give the doors a push. They move a bit, but don't open.

"So now the problem is Suzy," I say, because I know Inge won't leave her bike outside, but then Inge gives the doors a hard shove and they open.

Inge goes to fetch her bike and I go to fetch my packs. We cross the school grounds and we are aware that we are visible in the waning light to any villagers who might be watching, so we quickly and quietly get the bike into the school and close the doors.

Once inside we can hear a truck cruising slowly past the back side of the school where the construction trailer is, and we see it through the windows and we duck.

"Do you think they saw us?" Inge whispers. I shrug.

The truck stops and someone gets out of it. We hear voices, and we hold our breath, smiling at each other with wide eyes, but after a few minutes they get back into the truck and drive away.

I show Inge the room with the mattresses. For some reason she flips a light switch, and it works—the lights come on—and then she quickly turns the switch back off so as not to alert the village that there are intruders in their village school.

"Maybe I can block the window," I say, and for the next ten minutes I arrange a mattress to cover the window and rags to fill in the cracks.

I turn on the light and Inge creeps out the door to check it. She can see the light shining through cracks in the window despite my efforts but we use the light anyway when we need it. In the meantime we have our headlamps.

In silence we arrange our kitchen on a table in the hallway. I prepare the tomatoes and the garlic while Inge boils the spaghetti on her cooking stove. After draining the hot water on the floor she adds what I've prepared with some olive oil and she gives me half of the pasta in my green plastic bowl and we have our dinner.

We then retire to our little room, where we each have a double mattress bed. We stay up for a while chatting about our time in Edirne and about the news we saw in a teahouse of snow in Istanbul, and then we sleep well in our sleeping bags on mattresses. Before dawn the muezzin's call to prayer awakens us and we have already had our Turkish coffee and gotten back on the road by the time the sun comes up.

In the village there is a dog—there is always a dog—and it comes to Inge, and Inge loves it up in a way that no human will ever know, and we leave the village and where the village ends it is the end of the world. We are back on the plains that are like the sea—we have been on these plains for several days—on this sea—and we are pitching ourselves into the swells that are the long, endless ridges.

Inge cycles ahead, pushing straight up the next ridge. Then she slows, struggling, weaving serpentine, and finally dismounting near the top where she waits for me. I plod onward, leaning into the barren ridge. When I reach the top I take a short break, sitting on my backpack and smoking and having a drink from my water bottle, but Inge is impatient because she has already been waiting for me for several minutes, and as I begin again Inge swoops down the ridge on Suzy and she's a third of the way up the next ridge before she slows and weaves serpentine, then walks her bike to the top. I just plod along, steady, slow.

A power plant rises from the sea up ahead—far away—on the horizon—yet it takes no time at all to reach it—an hour—maybe two hours. I have been walking for over 14 months, and that time walking has culminated in finding myself beneath a power plant's ominous towers. Inge and I stop to smoke, but the towers have no smoke coming out of them. There is no sign of life.

Beyond the power plant we pass a dump—a ridge of garbage along the dirt track. There are two massive grey puppies on the rubbish heap, rooting for a meal. We pause to look at the abandoned dogs. Inge pushes out her lower lip—she wants to save them—but we move on, into the next trough, and to the peak of the next swell.

There is a lone tree, and I photograph it.

We come to another village, an island in the sea, and pause for a break. Inge briefs me on the navigational possibilities. We can continue the long way, away from the big roads, or take the shorter route on the highway. We choose the long way on the rough dirt road across the sea and over the swells. We roll cigarettes and we smoke, and we survey the view of the village below with its mosque with the Estes rocket minaret, and dirt roads with deep ruts leading to the next ridge. A local couple is curious—they meander towards us over clods of clay—we wave, say ‘Merhaba’—they do the same—we move on.

That night we are near a village and before the village there is another abandoned school but this one is beyond renovation—it is a ruin—and we pitch a tent inside it, under what is left of the roof because there may be rain. It takes 20 minutes to clear the floor of rubble to make space for the tent—it takes me another 15 minutes to gather wood for a fire. Some of the villagers watch as I gather fallen branches from a tree on the grounds but I don't care. I make the fire near the corner wall in our ruin and the cracks in the wall widen from the heat and I wonder if the whole thing will come down on us but I take no action to prevent it. The cracks widen in the wall, the plaster buckles, we eat, we sleep, we rise with the muezzin, we move on. It is all good.

We come to a town around lunch time. Inge does the shopping in a grocery store while I watch her bike. When she comes out, she is excited.

“Do you still want shoes?” she asks.

I have been wearing snow boots since Serbia, but they are terrible to walk in now that there is no snow.

“They have walking shoes for 14 Lire,” she says.

“That’s about 7 Euros,” I say.

“Ya.”

“I’ll check,” I say.

Inside I find the bin full of shoes and I find brown walking boots in my size and I buy them, and when I come outside a woman from the store comes out to smoke, and she watches as I remove my snow boots and put on my new walking shoes—it is a happy moment for me but also for Inge—this simple moment—and the woman goes inside and returns with instant coffee for us, and now it is a happy moment for all three of us.

Back on the plain—on the sea—and though the swells are smaller now the wind has not abated. The previous town is over the horizon behind us, the next one has yet to appear on the horizon before us.

Inge has cycled ahead, and on the dirt track in the distance a cart approaches, pulled by a trotting mule. In this world I can see only the plain and this approaching cart and I can hear only the wind and my own breathing. I stop to unload my packs, and I untie my snow boots and remove them from my big pack, and as the cart nears me it's driver peers—he is dark and stocky, middle aged, with a thick crop of gray hair blown by the wind—we are the only humans in existence—and I stand and wave the boots at him and he slows the cart, not stopping it—and he shakes his head—he thinks I am selling them—but I thrust the boots towards him and as he passes he takes the boots and then he lightly whips the mule back to speed and waves without looking back and I haul my packs back onto my body and I plod onward expecting to find Inge somewhere beyond the next ridge.

After some time there is a car—it is the only car—and it speeds down the low ridge but I can only hear the wind. Only when it has passed through the trough and rises towards me do I hear the car's motor, and as I and the car are the only two things on the sea, it stops beside me. The man in the car laughs and asks me questions and though I don't understand the language I know what the questions are.

"Istanbul!" I shout above the motor and the wind.

"Istanbul?" he shouts back, and something else, but I shrug.

The man hands me a can of beer and speeds away across the sea. I unload my packs and sit on the big pack and I gulp down the beer and I belch loudly and after cursing because the wind makes it hard to light my cigarette. I smoke and I observe the barren land and I know Inge is waiting beyond that ridge but I want this moment smoking and drinking beer alone with God and I take it and I am a happy madman.

The plain flattens—the sea levels out, though the wind has not abated. The road is gravelly asphalt now, and it straightens, and there is a dog, and it has found Inge, and she loves it, and we move on, and the dog follows behind for a bit, then stands on the plain, watching us go.

A short time later we pass a creek and its edges are iced over. The wind moans. We push forward. This is our work—pushing forward. We are huddled up and I plod while Inge cycles slowly ahead and it is a melancholy scene and I am in love with this life.

Late in the day we approach a village. There is another closed school at the edge of the village but this school is not under construction—it is merely closed—and it is next to a teahouse.

Inge has parked her bike next to a statue of a man who isn't Ataturk and she walks to the school building and pushes on the door and peers into a window.

"Not a good idea!" I shout. "Not very discreet here, Moots."

"I don't give a fuck! It's cold!"

A pudgy little man scurries past and he points at Inge and wags his finger. He scurries into the teahouse.

"Okay, now the village is being alerted," I shout.

"I don't give a fuck!" she repeats.

I sit at the base of the statue of the man who isn't Ataturk and roll a cigarette and I sigh. Inge is pushing on windows.

A man comes out of the teahouse, followed by the pudgy little fellow. The pudgy fellow stops at the door of the teahouse but the other man walks towards me. He is a man in his thirties with a thin moustache. He is wearing a worn, brown suit with a striped pullover underneath. He has a brown military cap on his head. It resembles the visored caps Japanese soldiers wore in World War 2. There is a patch with a big star on the cap. There is an emblem of authority on his suit. He seems to be a village security man. He stands in front of me, watching Inge walk around to the back of the school. I sit at the base of the statue of the man who isn't Ataturk and smoke. I am at the security man's mercy. I am smiling. The man is not smiling though, and he gestures toward Inge, then shrugs.

"I don't know," I say. "Yeah, it's cold; we need a place to stay. We need a place to sleep out of the cold."I put my hands together, tilt my head, and put my hands against my cheek. Sleep.

The man wags his finger. He pulls a cigarette out from a pack and lights it. He seems to be thinking. Then he beckons for me to come. As I go with him, Inge returns.

"Ya, I couldn't find a way in," she says.

"Okay, well, I'm being arrested," I say. "See you later. Watch my bags."

The man leads me up some steps behind the tea house. He leads me into a large room, then into a small room which seems to be a doctor's office. There is an exam table, and a screen to separate it from the rest of the office. The security man extends his hand. He points to Inge outside, then to the floor of the office, then he gestures that we can sleep here. I gesture myself to confirm it, he nods. I clasp my hands together and say, "Tershekular!"

The man waves off my thanks. He pats a portable heater and nods. Then he points downstairs and gestures eating and drinking. I thank him again. We both descend the steps and he returns to the teahouse. I walk to where Inge is, smoking by her bike. She watches me closely as I approach.

"Okay, we have a place to stay tonight," I say smiling. "A doctor's office or something. It's got a heater. Also, there's food."

Inge smiles back.

# Glastonbury, England

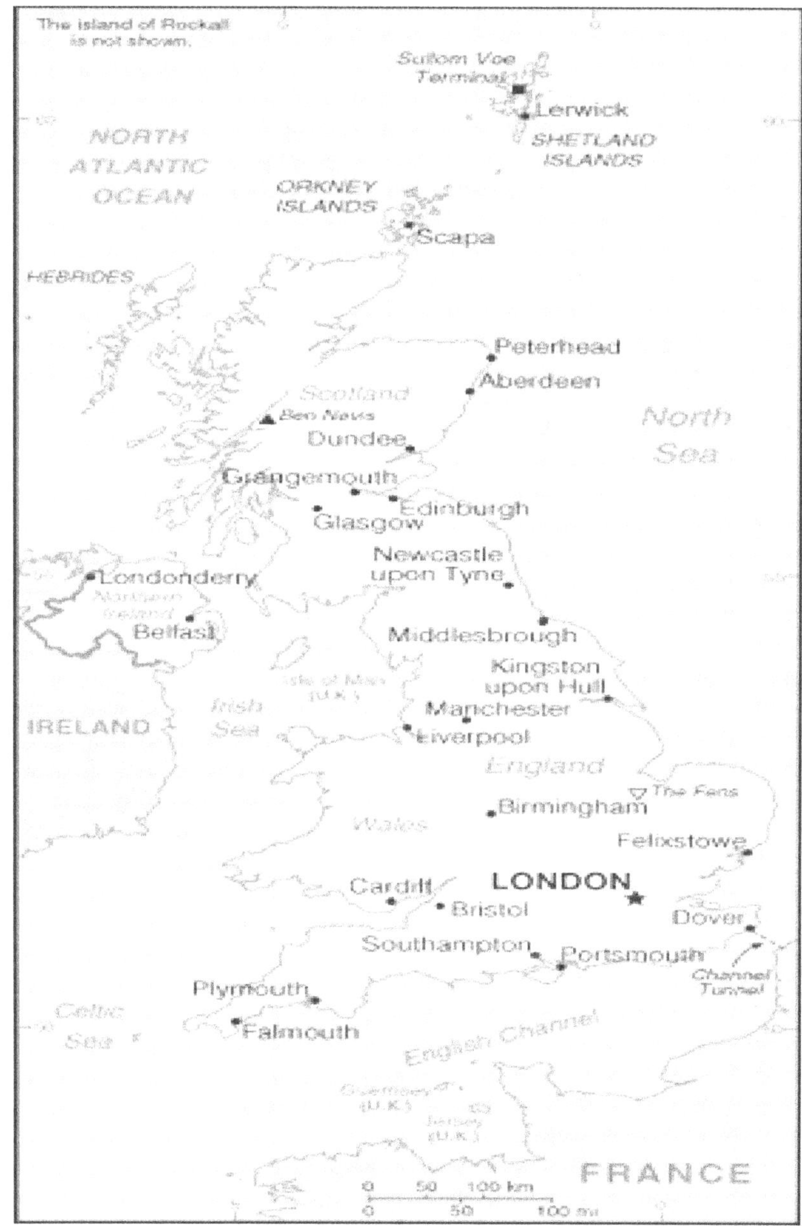

# Tiera St. Claire

Tiera's writing and poetry comes from an innate connection to her emotional experience. After divorcing 10 years ago, Tiera has been travelling in Europe, England, California, Maui, New York and Sedona. She writes when something catches her eye, touches her heart or engages her passions. Embracing the life of a pilgrim, Tiera walked the Camino Santiago in northern Spain 5 times, journaling her thoughts, feelings and experiences along the way.

You can find her or follow her on Facebook as Tiera St Claire

Her blog is **tierastclaire.com**

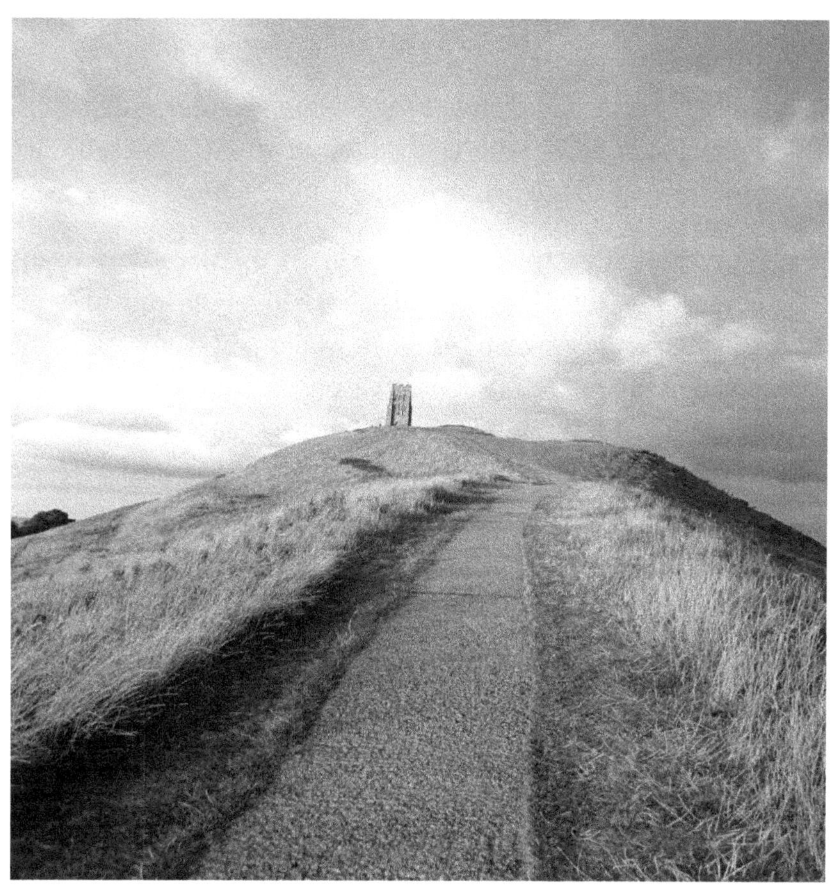

# Three Reasons to visit Glastonbury

By

**Tiera St. Claire**

Glastonbury is oft visited by those seeking connection to the Arthurian Legends, those who fancy themselves goddesses, those looking for healing and to do deep soul work.

These are valid reasons to go anywhere in my opinion. (Yes, even the Arthurian bit.) But Glastonbury is also a lovely town with delightful shops and cafes. So for those who might be travelling with someone going for one of the above reasons but really would, yourself, just like a brief holiday I offer these:

Take photos of the doors

Shop at the Charity Shops

and what was the third? Oh yes...

Climb the Tor and/or go to the Chalice Well

The doors in Glastonbury are not more spectacular, per se, than other doors in other quaint towns throughout Britain, but there are some lovely ones and even some engaging shop names to photograph as well. The Psychic Piglet is gone since I was there last, but there is still Enlightenment, The Goddess and the Greenman, Cat and Cauldron and Burns the Bread.

And the Charity shops are fantastic. Along with your everyday collection of clothes, books and household items, you can find crystals, Tarot cards and goddess paraphernalia.

I save the Tor and Chalice Well for last, and they are the best. You can see the Tor, rising proudly yet humbly from miles around, with the Tower of St Michael atop it.

I'd like to claim that I am not a fanciful type and yet felt the energy of this place anyway. Except that I am a fanciful type. That does not take away from the simple power this mount holds. I, quite honestly, was transported back in time when first I walked upon the Tor. I could see myself as a young girl, belonging to the land, running wild before I would take my vows to the goddess. But I have always imagined myself with a connection to Ancient Avalon.

The Chalice Well is, truly, an oasis of peace. The gardens are lovely and well maintained, the Well is available to behold and there is a small wading pool to walk through – it is very cold! Here, again, I felt the Spirit of the Land welcoming me home, saying I would be always welcome.

Do check out the lovely Chalice Well gift shop before you leave. It is small and filled with crystals and cards, jewelry and vibrational essences. We browsed the divination decks (they have open ones so you can ask those burning questions) tried on a couple of rings, bought some gold coins and fresh pressed apple juice made from apples growing in the garden. Delicious!

Around the corner from the Chalice Well gardens, there are founts where you can fill up bottles (that you've brought) with water from the 2 wells – one iron rich, called the Red Spring and one calcium rich, called the White Spring. The water is fresh and lovely and deeply nourishing.

Afterwards we had a scone and coffee at a cafe on the High Street called La Terre. The scone was excellent, the coffee not so much.

If you want a good cup of coffee, the best I have found in England is in Canterbury. But that is another story altogether.

**_I Gave Myself to You_**

*It was a gift of passion*
*It was a gift of love*
*A gift freely given*
*Requires no reward*

*This heart of mine*
*Beats with such passion*
*These hands touch with love and tenderness*
*This mind runs wild and free*
*Yet comes to the call of a soul connection*

*I see you*
*I recognize you*
*I know you*

*Your eyes beheld mine*
*In the beginning of Time*
*Your sword guarded the Mysteries*
*My Chalice eased the parched lips of the Seekers*
*We stood before the Grail*
*Held council with the Ancient Ones*
*And said when the time comes*
*We will be ready*

*Whom does the Grail serve?*
*The Grail serves the Grail King*

*The Grail King serves the Land*
*The Queen calls the King to hold court as the Land awakes*

*The New Day dawns*
*The Mysteries are revealed*

*I remember standing before the Grail*
*In a circle of Nine*
*Chanting*
*As the curtain of Time*
*Set upon us the veil of forgetfulness*
*The Grail has been held by the Spirit of Truth*
*In Time out of time*
*The Circle has remained unbroken*
*For we have been chanting and holding the hand of Truth*
*From that moment to this*
*And the blink of an eye has awoken us from the Trance*

*Was it your eye who woke up first*
*Or was it mine?*

*I find myself here*
*Wedded to the 3rd dimension*
*Tears streaming down my face*

## *Heart rent asunder*

*For you have forsaken me*
*Before you remembered who I Am*

*And I*
*Soul of power and love*
*Heart of passion and fire*
*Live in this feeling body*
*Who is coming awake*
*Channeling vast cosmic forces*
*And looking for an anchor of love*

*Forgive me*

*I thought you were that anchor*
*I thought you were that love*
*The memory of Union*
*The joy of surrender*
*The sweet, sweet nectar of bliss*
*Outweighed your words of separation*

*To once again know the soul filling contentment*
*Of offering my allegiance*
*Queen of the Mysteries to Grail King*
*Was so seductive*
*That I lay myself before you*
*Before you were ready to receive me*

*The pain of a shattered heart is almost too much to bear*
*And not nearly so great as the pain of betraying the Truth*

*The Truth lives in me*
*I Am a Keeper of the Grail*
*I hold the Mysteries of Love*
*And now my heart has been broken open*
*So the mysteries can be revealed*

*I sing the song of Creation*
*I open my heart to Love*
*I intone the sacred Word*
*I pour the Grail Codes upon thirsty land*
*And feel the hungry Earth as She awakes*

*Behold*
*Freedom's call has sounded*
*Wake up now*

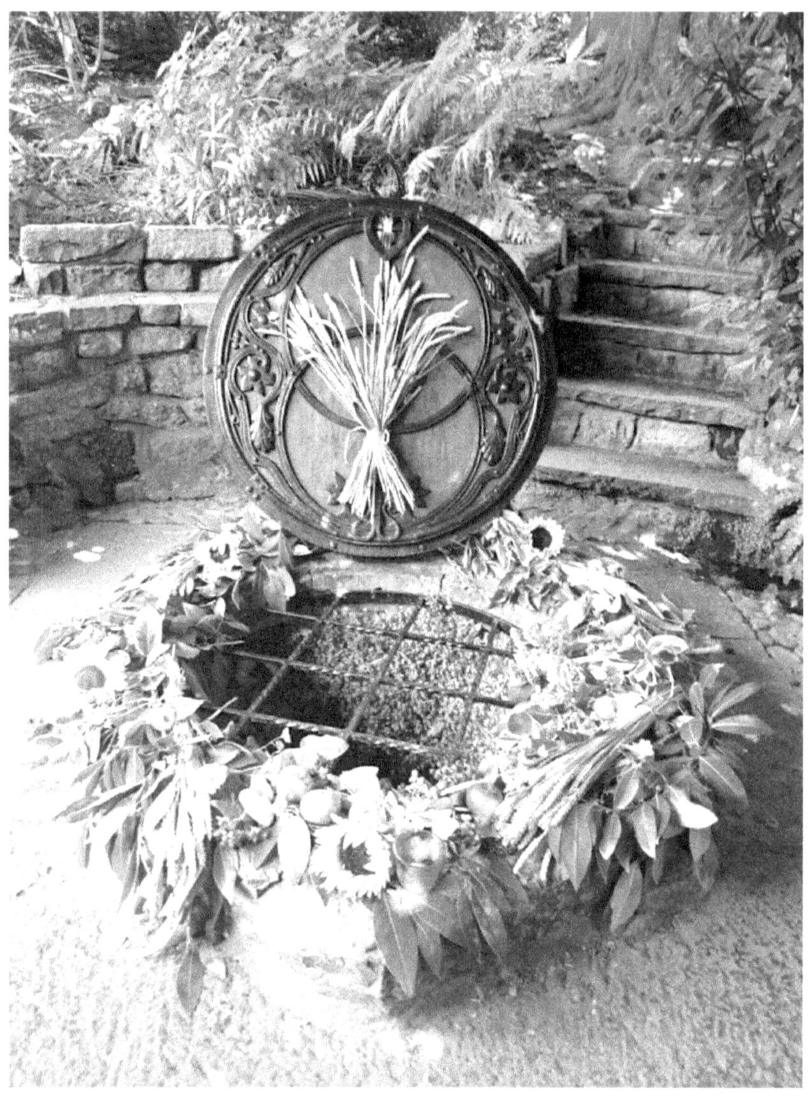

The Chalice Well

# New Zealand

New Zealand
National capital
Railroad
Expressway
Road
Ferry
Norfolk Island (AUSTRALIA)
KERMADEC ISLANDS
THREE KINGS ISLANDS
North Island
NEW ZEALAND
CHATHAM ISLANDS
South Island
BOUNTY ISLANDS
SNARES ISLANDS
AUCKLAND ISLANDS
ANTIPODES ISLAND GROUP
Campbell Island
North Cape
Te Kao
SOUTH PACIFIC OCEAN
Whangarei
Dargaville
Tasman Sea
Great Barrier Island
Waitakere
North Shore
Auckland
Manukau
Tauranga
East Cape
Hamilton
Whakatane
Rotorua
Taupo
Gisborne
New Plymouth
Cape Egmont
Hawera
Hastings
Napier
Wanganui
Cape Farewell
Palmerston North
Collingwood
Karamea
Picton
Nelson
Lower Hutt
Wellington
Westport
Blenheim
Cape Palliser
Reefton
Greymouth
Hokitika
Kaikoura
Christchurch
Whataroa
Akaroa
Haast
Ashburton
Banks Peninsula
Timaru
Milford Sound
Oamaru
Alexandra
Middlemarch
Te Anau
Dunedin
West Cape
Gore
Invercargill
Solander Island
Stewart Island
BOUNTY ISLANDS

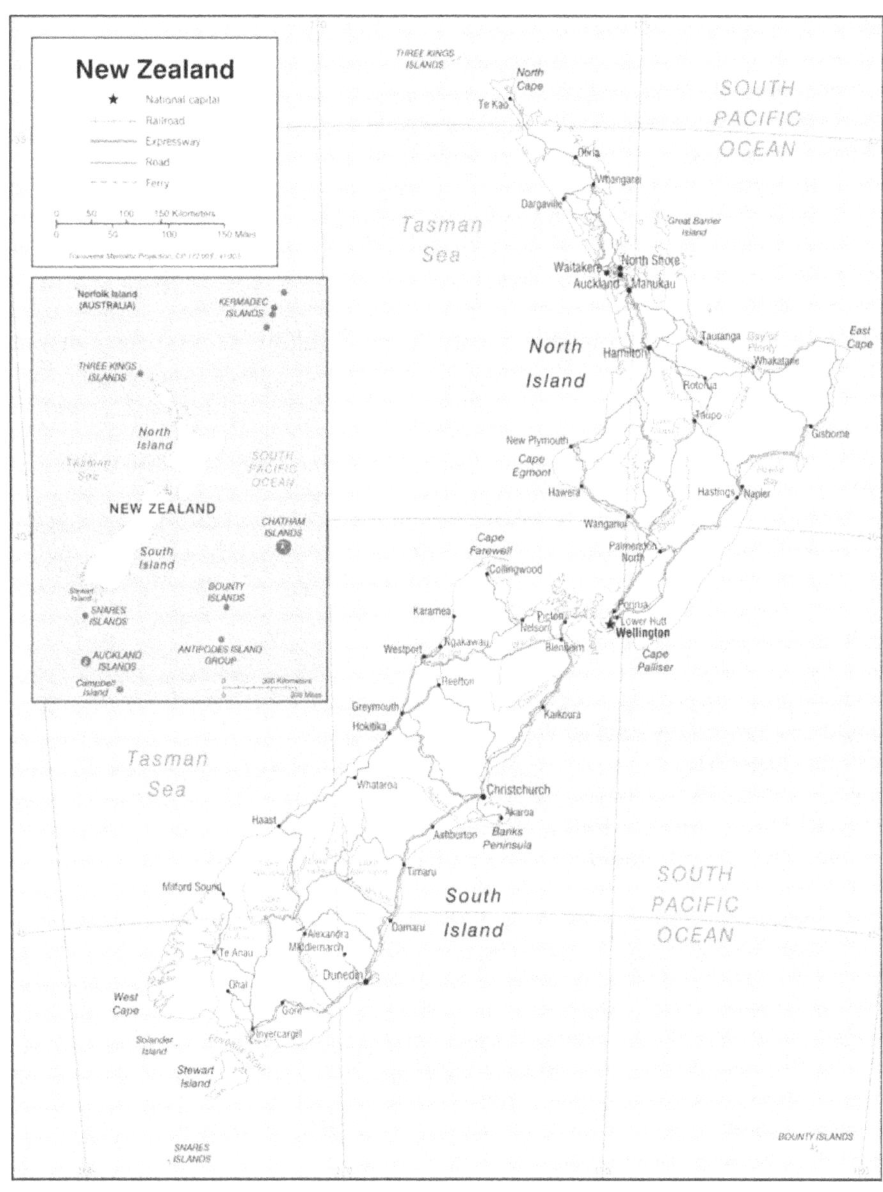

# Robin Hall

Robin Hall is a neo-Renaissance man: A life coach, writer and narcissist in recovery. He uses humor and storytelling to encourage people to move towards a healthy, happy, and more meaningful lifestyle. His depth and wisdom are extraordinary. Robin is a Kiwi (as in a New Zealander, not a piece of fruit) who lives in Los Angeles.

Links:

Website: www.facebook.com/kiwitrainer
Blog: I Love Me
Facebook: www.facebook.com/kiwitrainer
Twitter: https://twitter.com/thelegendofr
Youtube Channel: https://www.youtube.com/user/RobinJHall

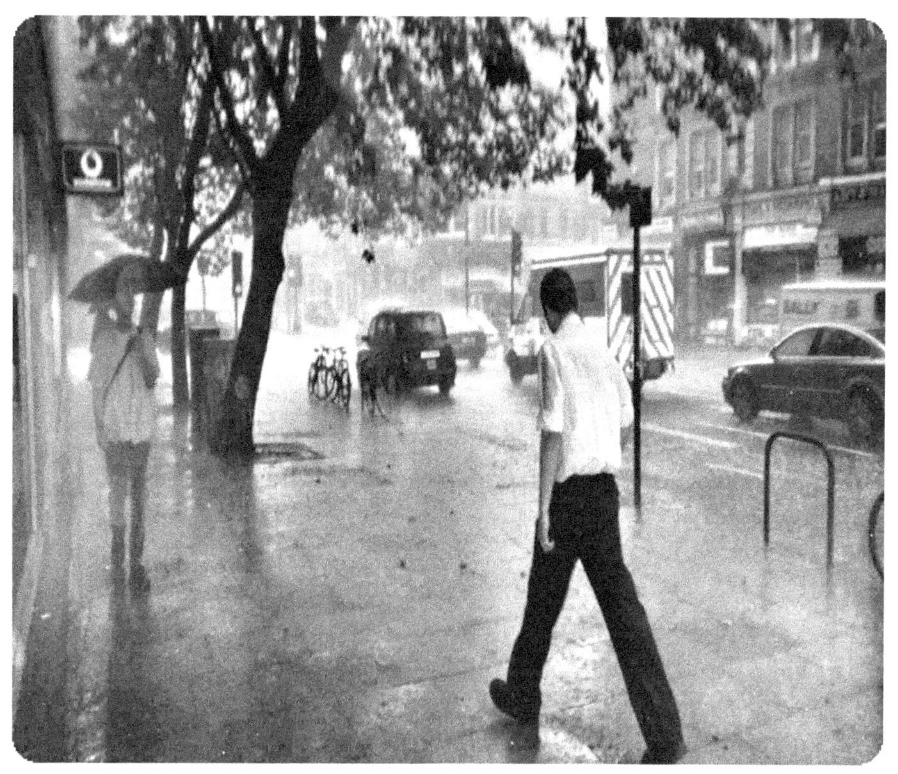

# The London Weather

By:

**Robin Hall**

## Robin Hall

A dark and foreboding mood swept into my soul just as my lunch break beckoned. I strategically decided to take a cigarette break right before my officially scheduled one so that I could effectively squeeze out a couple of extra minutes of downtime.

A thick drizzle had settled in during the morning, which was not altogether surprising considering London's usual climate; which is predominantly soggy. To protect myself a little from the rain, I crammed myself into a corner with a small overhang. It was in the alleyway that lay adjacent to the clothing store where I worked as a salesman. There were restaurants across the way, and also, a dance studio. I took a few furtive glances into the dance studio like a proper pervert at the ladies tearing it up on the dance floor in their leotards. Today wasn't a day for trifling fantasy though. There was something sad going on up there in the cosmos. Tragedy was hanging thick in the air.

You know that irksome feeling when something true is worrying you? It is a sense deeper than your average run of the mill paranoia, a sensible and quiet sadness grounded in truth. When I went into our break room and took out my phone there was a message from my cousin, whose floor I was sleeping on. She was wondering if I had seen Tapper, her recent ex-boyfriend. He had gone missing. My heart dropped. Something bad had indeed happened, I just had that sense of inescapable dread. A sick feeling sat in my gut for the rest of the afternoon.

A thick, very depressing cloud of worry and darkness followed me home that evening. The actual weather mirrored my internal state rather well, it was a good example of my old friend pathetic fallacy. I walked in the front door of my flat and into a picture of grief; A community had gathered, a wake had begun.

I was informed that Tapper had been found hanging from a set of swings in the playground of the local park. My cousin was distraught. Destroyed and devastated she cried her lungs out and wailed in anguish. She was comforted, joined and surrounded by a caring crew of close friends.

Tapper was a bright spirit and had a giant smile that was unbelievably wide. He was always very generous and welcoming to me and I could always count on him to share with me one of his Marlboro Reds, a real cigarette; a good meal of tobacco those Marlboro Reds. It was a sad tragedy and although I felt it and it hurt and I was in shock, I wasn't part of the inner circle so to speak, the close family of friends that had gathered in the living room, the room that doubled as my current bedroom.

I sat there on the couch watching this incredible community bond together and share in the grief, comforting one another. I was always made welcome by this crew, but never in my short time knowing them, did I feel like I became one of them.

They just were not pretentious enough for me, a tad too genuine and real, a bunch of down to earth Kiwis, Aussies and South Africans. I needed to be surrounded by fellow self-obsessed narcissists at that stage of my life. They were lovely but I didn't feel completely comfortable with them, or myself at that time in my development for that matter.

Donboy, one of the crew and a close friend of my cousins, came and sat next to me on the couch. He gently began to converse with me in a settled, caring and well thought out manner,

"Ancella is really cut up. We are probably going to be grieving and based here all night. Maybe there's gonna be people crashing in this room for a couple of days and nights. She doesn't feel comfortable with you having you, you know, be around all this. Do you have a friend you can stay with for a while?"

"Yeah", I nodded. It was a tad strange and awkward me being there. I did feel a little like an outsider. Death and grief are intimate events. I smiled, quickly packed together a backpack with a few changes of clothes and quietly made my way back out onto the London streets and into the wet night.

The truth was I had no friends or nowhere to stay and I was pretty broke. I knew no-one else in London, well, that was not entirely true. I dialed Fedor. Fedor was a man who may or may not have been homeless. I knew he drank, wrote poetry and I also knew his telephone number. I called him.

I explained the situation to Fedor and then asked the pertinent question.

"So, umm, whereabouts do you ahh, stay?"

"Well I am in a state housing apartment". Wait, he wasn't homeless? Hope sprung from its eternal well.

"Would it be possible for me to stay with you? Not for long. maybe a day or two?"

"Yes, O.K. I don't have much. I live in a state housing apartment".

"Oh anything is great. Anything. Thank you so much".

I was overjoyed. I jumped on the train and headed his way. Here he was, an almost complete stranger, almost homeless, who at the drop of his scrungy hat, was going to let me crash at his place. I was elated by the generosity of his spirit and swiftly made my way through the oppressively wet night with a heavy but grateful heart. It was a sad day, but I had a roof over my head and so it wouldn't at least be a sad wet night. I felt comforted.

The state housing complexes rise up like soulless fortresses; plain brick facades upon plain brick facades. There was a call box type entry system that looked like it had been made by the same company that manufactures those phone systems in prison. It probably was. There was something of a penitentiary about the whole thing, a prison of poverty if you will. But at least this was free housing. People with little means had a solid structure and roof over their heads. That's a good society.

Fedor buzzed me up. He was moping and melancholic but very hospitable. He showed me a room with a large patent-leather chair, with an old, synthetic covering scabby and picked at. The chair rocked back and you could recline in it, thus it served the purpose of a bed too. The room was pretty bare. The only other object was a computer, circa nineteen-eighty something, sitting atop a very stark chair and desk. It continued the theme of the design, the captivity aesthetic boasted by the exterior of the building had been carried into the interior expertly. It brought the outside in. At least the design theme was consistent.

“Do you want a bath?” Fedor lazily queried.

“That would be incredible”. It would be.

“Oh. That is going to be a problem. I don’t have any hot water, but I can heat some in a pot. I never use the bath”.

“That would be great”. I smiled. I had been chilled on the way over. The thought of any type of warm bath thrilled me.

Over the next twenty minutes, Fidel heated water in a small pot over a single flame gas burner. I ferried it to the bath when it had reached a boiling point.

The low bulbs gave the feeling that we were living in the last light cast at the end of a battery powered torches life; you know when it begins to give up the ghost and the beam wanes to a pathetic, orange glow where once it had been blindingly stark, white and bright. It was an unhealthy, anemic illumination that highlighted, or more accurately low-lighted, the stark sterility of poverty.

There was little conversation between me and Fedor. He slowly sipped from a bottle of red wine and continued with deep fascination the apparently mesmerizing business of heating the water.

“I do not usually have people over”. He philosophically confessed, staring off into the distance for a second, before returning his gaze back to that single, hypnotic flame.

Having secured a poor excuse for a bath, a good couple of inches of hot water, I excitedly took off my clothes, lowered myself into the shallows and began to spoon the delicious warm liquid over my body with the same pot that the water was heated and carried in.

A noble piece of cooking ware that pot was, It felt so damn awesome. I felt like I imagined a millionaire must feel: rich and happy and lucky. I sat there like a joyous child, playing with the water until I couldn’t pretend that the water had any warmth left in it whatsoever. Then I stayed just a little longer until there was no doubt that it was definitely cold.

I stepped out of the tub, vigorously toweled myself off, peeked into the kitchen, where Fidel had fallen asleep next to the blue gas flame. I quietly walked up and turned the burner off and then snuck into my room. I pulled out the sleeping bag, quickly hopped in it, as in a competitor at the start of a sack race, then bounced over to the well used red chair, slithered up on it, freed a single arm to loosen the back and reclined. I closed my eyes and gratefully let the sadness sink into my conscious like a low, melancholy lullaby.

Even the sunshine has a grey tinge in London. A stark light grey sunbeam cut through the cold winter morning air. There was no snow, but it felt like there was; it was as if you were existing in a giant industrial freezer. I wandered into work and began to count down the hours. I could not relax completely as Bajuetta was working. She was half West Indian and had perfect everything. I tried to play it cool and pretend I didn't notice she was pretty, but whenever I tried to be normal I freaked out, clammed up and began dithering, stammering and taking my innate awkwardness to exciting new highs. I could crack her up a little but most of the time just snuck quick peeks at her and marveled at how beautiful she was. She was, as they say, way out of my league and belonged on a fashion magazine cover.

On these cold cold days I often frequented a baked potato shop that was only a short walk down the smooth stoned, cobbled grey street. It was bright red, the inside seemingly inspired by an old school English telephone box.

There was something cozy and very comforting in a baked potato on a freezing London day. It just felt right and British to be greedily digging into a potato filled with cheese and whatever you had imagined might taste good. Those steaming hefty lumps of goodness provided both tremendous sustenance and also a second heat source.

They provided a nice supply of warmth it was transported spoonful by spoonful from the outside world into my grateful stomach which seemed to still retain some of the steaming heat a good half hour after the meal was over. Dark when the day started, dark when the day ended, no wonder they call it the London blues. The shock and sadness was still fresh. Tears gently sat back, letting you know they were ready to go at the slightest hair trigger. The day rolled by.

Dog tired I headed back to my temporary lodging. I removed the inmate phone from the scratched shiny steel call box and called up to Fedor's apartment. There was no answer. I tried a number of times over the next hour as well as repeated calls to his cell phone but to no avail. It did not look good. Strange, I thought. This guy was pretty dependable.

My cousin's place was out of the question. I could not by any means poke my head in to their grief after one night away. It was just not right. I did feel awkward again at going back to my sisters, since I did not want to offend her partner who had encouraged me to leave. I was in a bind though and again, had no place to stay. At least it wasn't snowing. It did however begin raining heavily.

Fuck. I called Emelia but she was not answering. Fuck. I was just going to have to swallow my pride, get onto the train and arrive at their doorstep, wet and bedraggled. She would understand and old Gustave would just have to be onerous and whiney behind closed doors all evening. I hurried to Kings Cross. I ran to the platform and looked at all the rows of red led lights only to read NO MORE TRAINS, next to the platform of the very one I needed.

I was apparently shit out of luck. But then I cast aside my tragic consequences and decided to fight fire with fire. I was going to fight the forces of melancholy by morphing into my superhero alter-ego Mr. Super Emo. It was time to take the Emo into overdrive.

My emo delusion was thus; I was a man beset on all sides by forces of sadness and had found himself alone, wet, and without a place to lay his weary head in a strange, unforgiving land. Would I settle for this? Would I take this lying down? Would I be able to find a spot to even lie in? So many questions, so much to get emo about.

In reality it was actually not the best situation, emo personas aside. It was very cold and it was raining hard and I need somewhere to stay. I was so wretchedly financially challenged that the prospect of getting even a cheap hotel room seemed like some reckless spending spree. I started walking into the hotels but apparently, London is a popular city and there were seemingly no rooms available. I got so wet that soon I could not even luxuriate in the fantasy that I was some lonely romantic hero. I was just plain miserable. I was in reality a drowned rat and there was no romance in that. I was cold, very cold and my one set of clothes was soaked to the bone.

After an hour or two I was becoming hot under the collar, figuratively, though I was literally blue with cold. I was pissed off and I was desperate. Finally there was a room at an Inn. A simple hotel, tidy and painted all in a sharp smart dark blue and adorned with terrible art with fake gold frames, overly ornate borders and various tacky, brassy furniture that filled out its interior. It felt very Faux Royal. I painfully parted with the nights rent and then headed to my room.

I closed the door to my room, quickly unrobed and headed straight for the shower. Steam and hot water flooded over my body. God it felt amazing. Bliss. Hot, hot water, more and more of it was flooding all over my face, hair and every bit of my body. It was luxury. It was heaven. It was as good as it gets.

I stepped out of the shower and grabbed a white fluffy towel and vigorously dried myself off, dropped the towel, walked over to the perfectly made bed, jumped on the bed and lay there naked feeling like a golden god. "I am pretty resilient", I said to myself as if I had undergone something of an epic trial, you know, something on the same level as that chap Nelson Mandela. It did feel really good though, lying there warm, clean and naked like a born again millionaire. I felt rich, powerful and most importantly grateful. Having a flair for the dramatic, I took a deep breath in and said out loud,

"I am resilient!"

"God, Robin, I'm sorry. I just started drinking from a bottle of red wine and forgot all about you." Fedor explained in melancholic monotones the next day.

"No problems, is it still okay to maybe stay for a night or two?"

"Yeah, yeah. I am sorry. I just started drinking and forgot you know? He confessed. I began to suspect Fidel had a drinking problem.

# Nathaniel Schellhase Hvizdos

Nathaniel Schellhase Hvizdos began his artistic career at an early age, making posters, flyers and backdrops for local bands in the Washington DC area. He went on to study Anthropology, Sociology and Film at Virginia Commonwealth University. Nathaniel's art displays images of fantastical creatures, skulls, animals, and more. In poetry, Nathaniel shows understanding of different perspectives as he explores various stories and emotions. He finds inspiration from miracles he sees around us. Current artwork at:

**www.nathanielschellhasehvizdos.com**

**www.Etsy.com/shop/HVIZDOS**

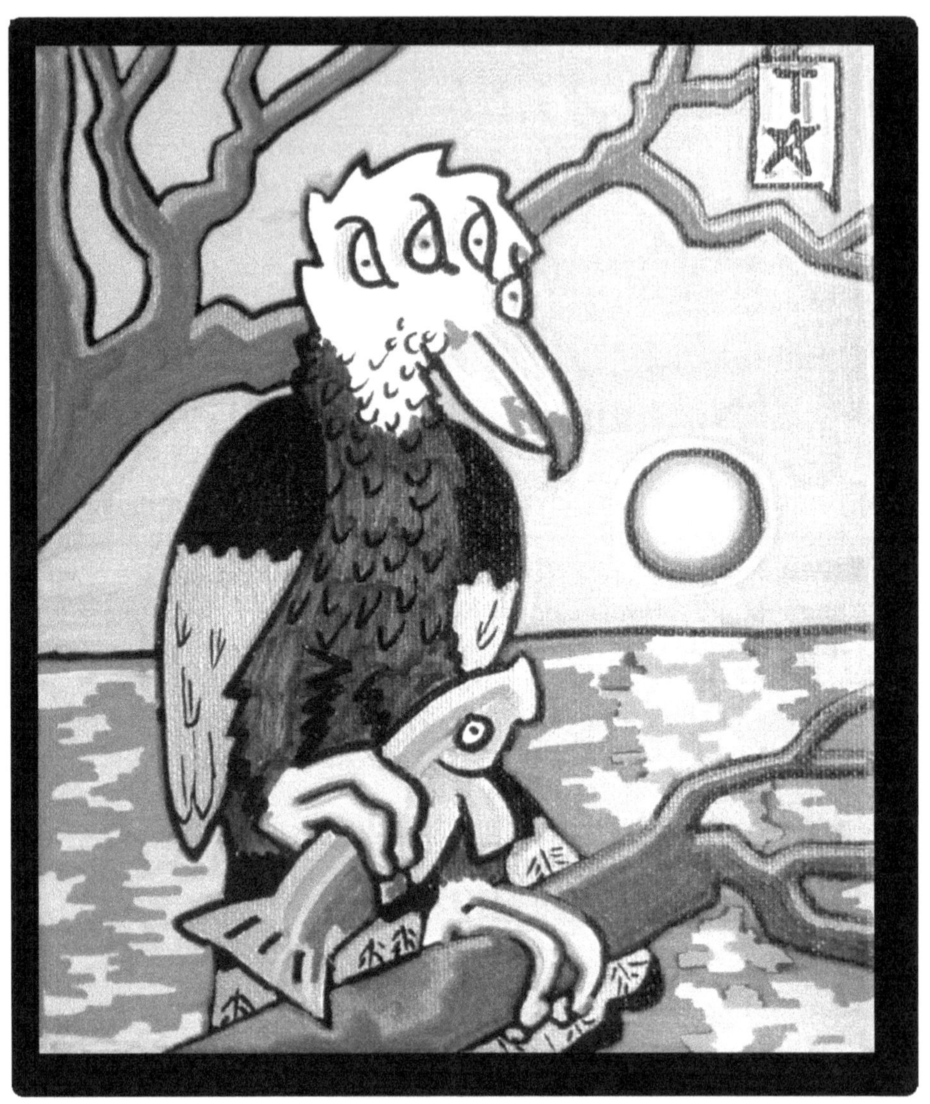

**Bird and Fish**

www.Etsy.com/shop/HVIZDOS

Nathaniel Schellhase Hvizdos

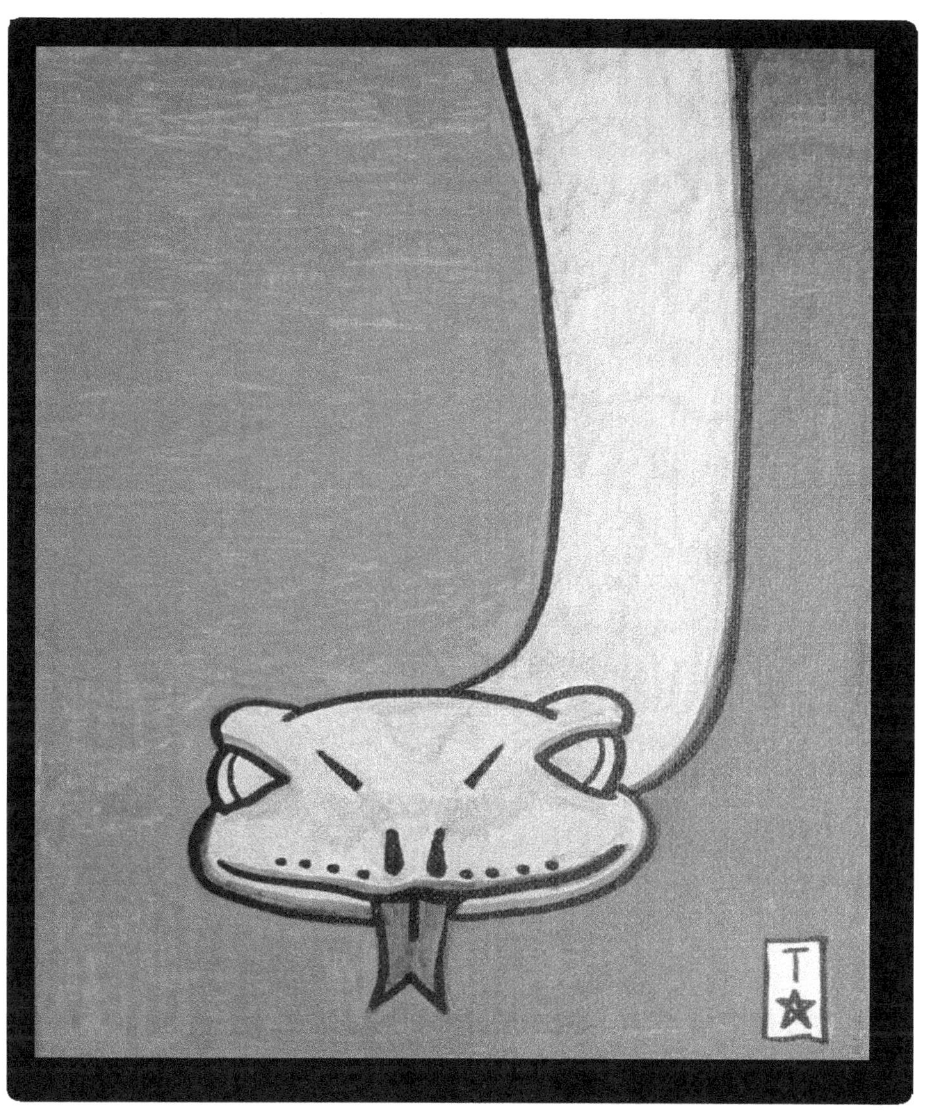

## Green Python

www.Etsy.com/shop/HVIZDOS

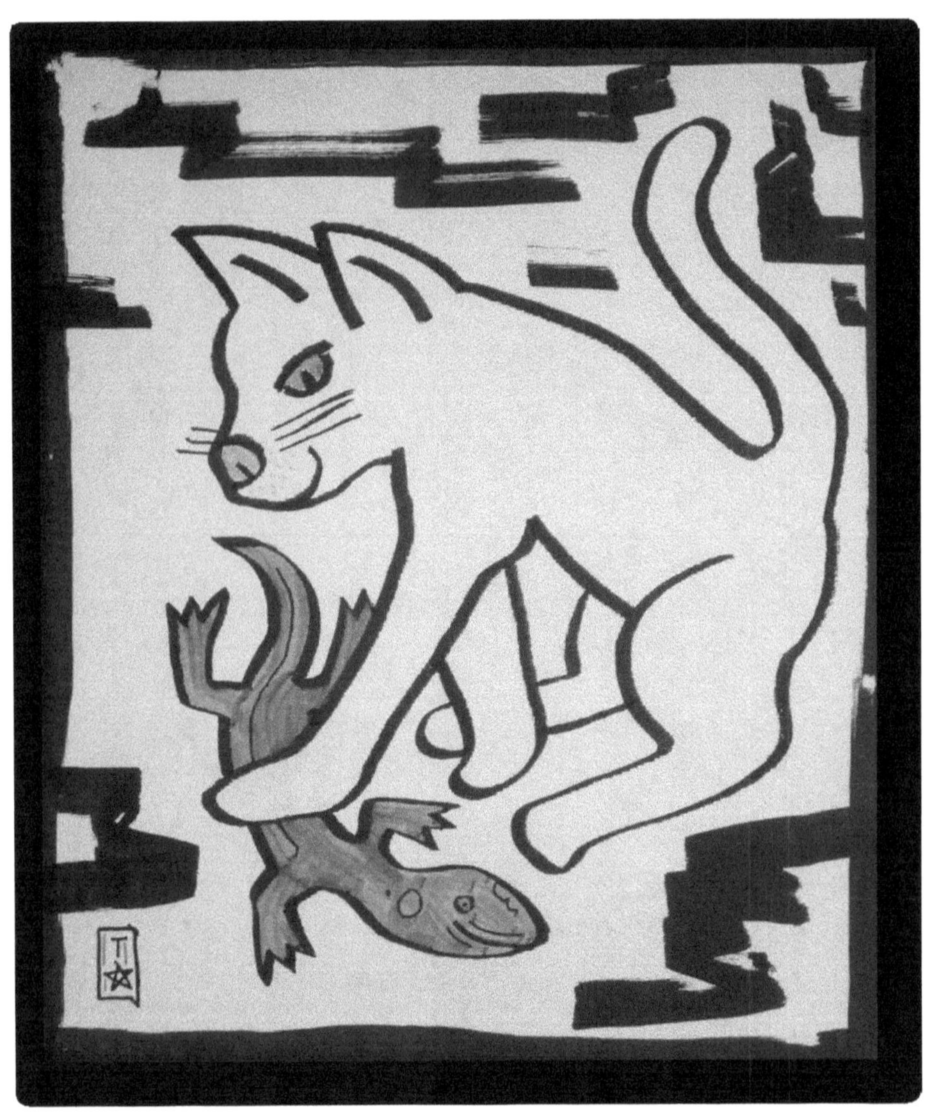

**Cat and Lizard**

www.Etsy.com/shop/HVIZDOS

Nathaniel Schellhase Hvizdos

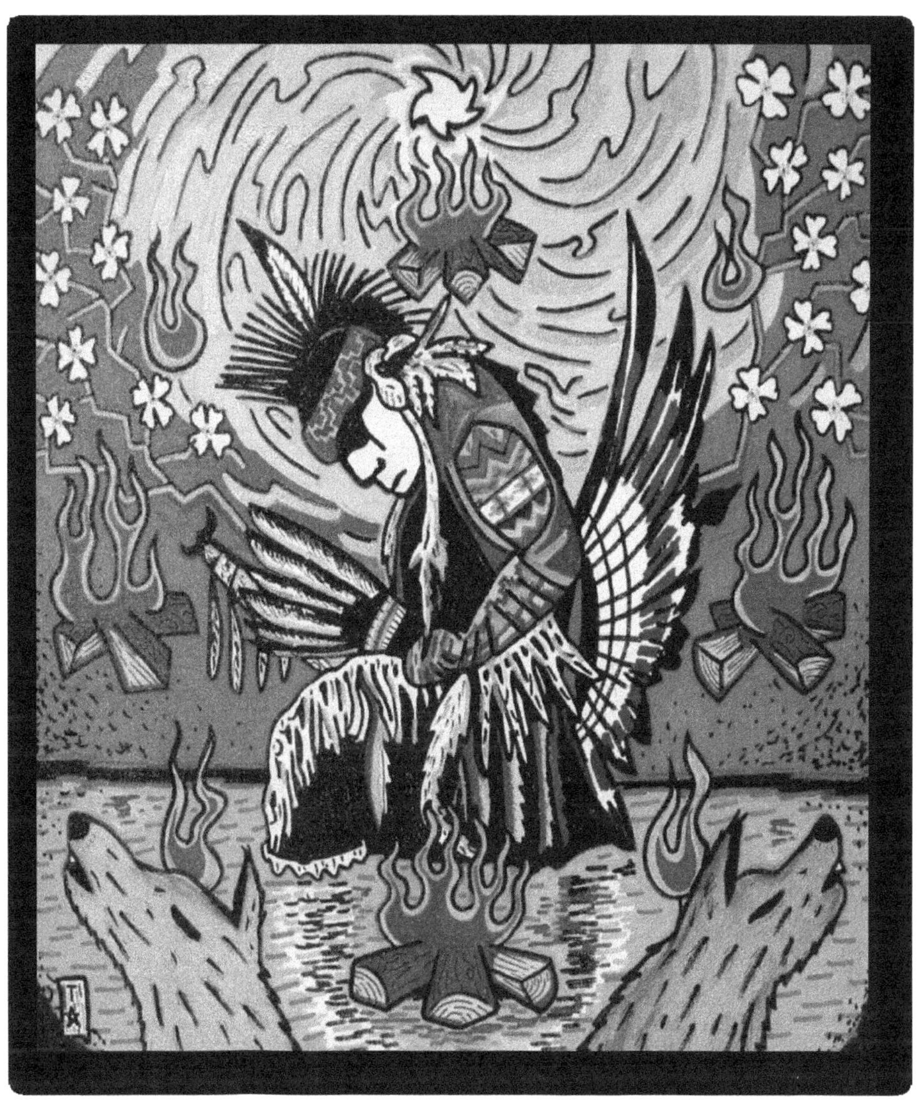

## The Guide

www.Etsy.com/shop/HVIZDOS

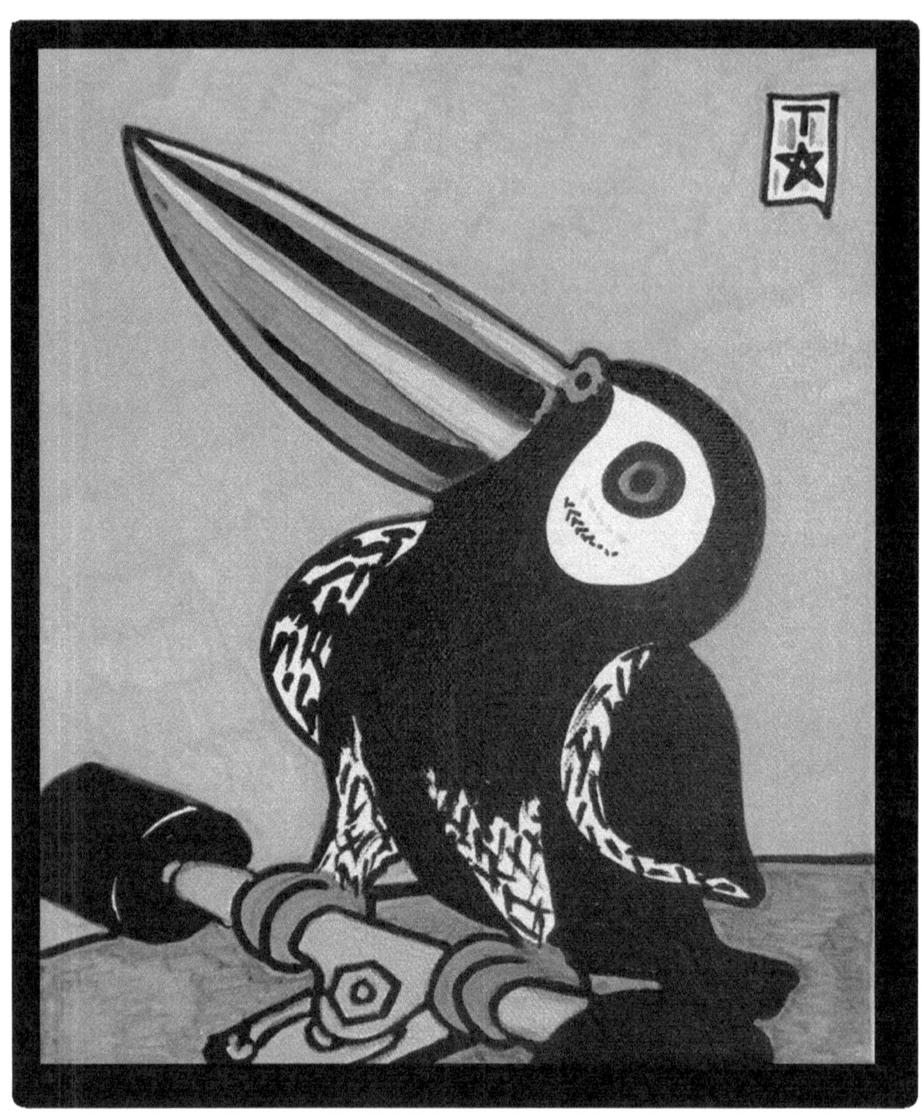

**Toucan**

**www.Etsy.com/shop/HVIZDOS**

# North Carolina

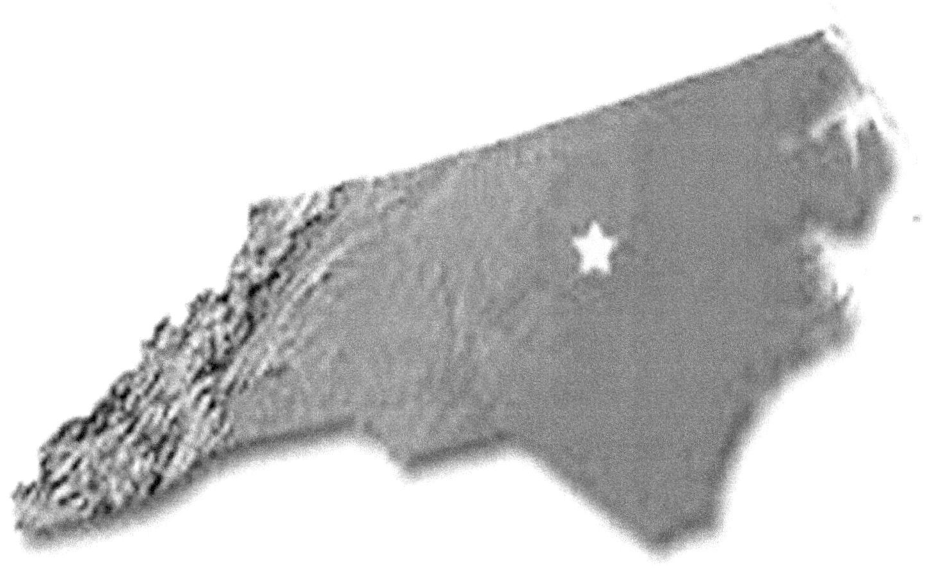

## N.K. Wagner

N.K. Wagner is the publisher and executive editor of Page & Spine, a weekly online literary magazine dedicated to promoting emerging writers.
Her work has appeared in print in several anthologies including:
Small Town Talk, Rewriters Press, 2008
Pen In Hand, 2009, Rewriters Press, 2009
Pen In Hand, 2010, Rewriters Press, 2010
Her poetry, short stories and essays can be read online at:
http://contemporaryhaibunonline.com/pages84/Wagner_CrackedBlock.html
http://www.pageandspineficshowcase.com
http://nkwagnerwriter.blogspot.com/
https://www.facebook.com/profile.php?id=100003341749080

N.K. Wagner

# SHELL-PATH

I contemplate my waning life
While walking ocean's foam.
Above me, on the sandy beach,
A shell-path points me home.

They're boring in their sameness, but
Amassed, they're still a sight.
These undistinguished corpses lie
Disgorged by ocean's might.

Then, there appears a won'drous thing.
Up through soft sand I trudge.
A special seashell beckons me
Whose quality I judge

Magnificent in form and hue.
No sameness have we here.
A work of art from God's own hand,
Indeed, it has no peer.

While I admire this lovely shell,
Unique among the rest,
I wonder: what I leave behind—
Will it pass my own test

Of a legacy worth leaving?
Will I stand out? I sigh.
I'm a shell within the shell-path—
A spec'men I'd pass by.

## WOODLAND WONDER

Through forest glade I wander
Toward the west'ring sun.
No hurry in my footsteps.
There's time 'fore day is done.

Each sunbeam spotlights something—
Some wonder to astound—
From rust'ling leafy ceiling
To fern-lace on the ground.

The air's alive with birdsong
And insects' throbbing buzz.
Just feel and smell the life here!
No place that ever was

Restores me like the woodland—
It feeds my weary soul,
Refreshes mind and Vision,
And leaves me feeling whole.

currently appears in Scribbles,

http://nkwagnerwriter.blogspot.com/

N.K. Wagner

## LOVERS' SPAT

He says, she says.
They mix it all around,
stir it up in separate bowls
and dump it on the ground.
But when they view
the mess they've made,
the pain they've brought to be,
they see there is no he or she—
there is only we.

## FOREVER FRIENDS

We're comfy together just like old shoes.
We're books of stories with differing views.
Our tastes complement: my tea and your toast.
No need to compete, no need to boast.
I brighten your day; you comfort my night.
You open windows; I welcome the light.
I pick my way caref'ly; you forge ahead.
Our journey's unique, when all's done and said.
If your tune and my words must disagree,
When storm clouds gather and winds lash our sea
We stop what we're doing, breathe deep, and then
Remember our friendship and start again
We're more together than each is alone.
Though we may wander, hearts know the way home.

N.K. Wagner

# SUBWAY SWING

Subway station busker blows
his clarinet at dawn.
His case holds scant donations.
People pause, but move on.
His melodies are timeless.
His breathing circles smooth.
His audience is sleeping…
Musician finds his groove.
He be-bops up their morning
As they scurry to the train.
Tiled walls echo his verses,
Tiled floors his scat refrain.
Supper money puddles deep
as trav'lers gather round.
Coins a silver torrent rain.
Scrip flutters gently down.
When rush hour crowds begin to thin
and hoard is hid away,
when lic'rice stick is safely stored,
Our student starts his day.

currently appears in scribbles,
http://nkwagnerwriter.blogspot.com/

# California

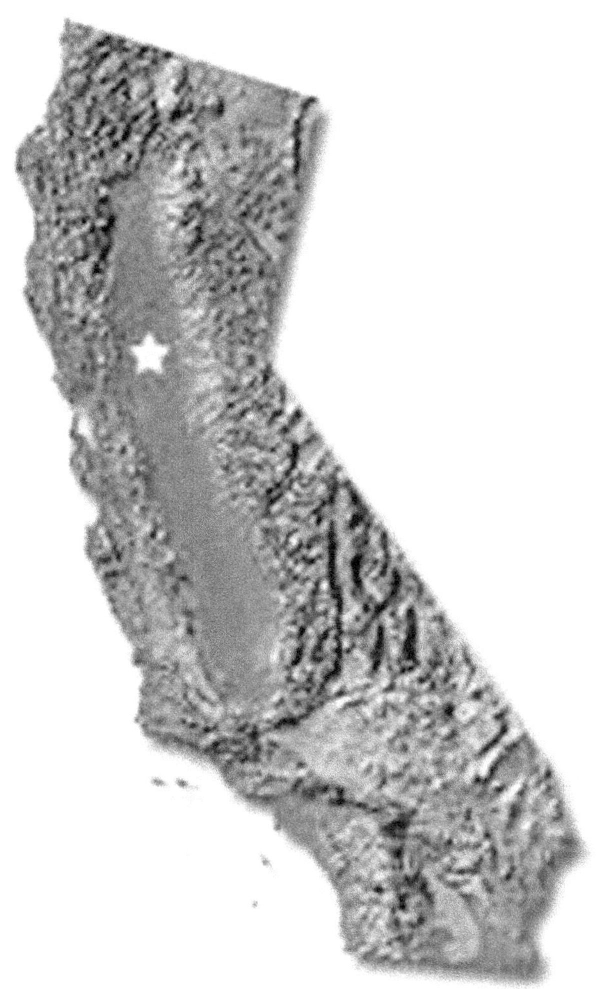

## Heather M. Browne

Dr. Heather M. Browne is a faith-based psychotherapist and recently emerged poet, published in the Orange Room, Boston Literary Review, Page & Spine, Eunoia Review, Poetry Quarterly, The Poetry Bus, Red Fez, The Muse, An International Journal of Poetry, Deep Water Literary Journal, Electric Windmill, Maelstrom, mad swirl, and Dual Coast. Her first chapbook, We Look for Magic and Feed the Hungry has just been published by MCI. She just won the Nantucket Poetry Competition and will be featured on their website. She has been married 20 years to her love, has 2 amazing teens, and can be found frolicking in the waves.

Follow her: www.thehealedheart.net

My poetry website is: www.thehealedheart.net
My chapbook is on sale on that site
or through Amazon, link:

http://www.amazon.com/We-Look-Magic-Feed-Hungry/dp/0993676952/ref=sr_1_1?s=books&ie=UTF8&qid=1402591838&sr=1-1&keywords=heather+browne

# Holding Me in Hug

Afraid - I wrap my arms 'round my legs - holding me in hug.
Struggling for your voice alone
You are gentle with my trembling.
And yet I shake. You lay your hand softly on my knee. I feel the start within.
But there's no slap with you.
And as I breathe deeply to settle shakiness, I feel the rock.
I rock - back and forth - back and forth. Wrapped - the embryo in womb.
How pathetically sad – how touchingly sweet
I breathe
waiting to be born.

# Kissing Death

Pink champagne lips smear
longing for hardened kisses
rosy cheeks smudge, resurrecting grey
her platinum curls gripping
still holding
She's laid out – lovely
amaranth satin sheets
we sit, ornately elegant chairs, rococo, feigning refinement
She's wearing pearls, by the way, tight around her saggy ears and neck
suffocating - lovely
They talk about how beautiful she looks

# Dead

I squirm and wrestle needing wind
to loosen her grip
meaning no disrespect in my need for free
As
Under
You raise your arm to slap
Quick to the floor I slide - counting
1 - 2 - 3
Your hand afflicts me - leaving me numb
"Damn it!  Forgive me," you say, reaching down with wedded hand
The one that strokes my breast and holds our child
Watching – screaming
Your anesthesia  thick – I can't, I can't  move
Your patience wearing thin - apology shallow
You grab me up yanking arm
Your ring leaving mark
Reminding me I am yours

"What therefore God hath joined together, let not man put asunder."
Definition :  Asunder: to pull apart, torn a
part into different parts or pieces
· in bits · in halves · in two

Heather M. Browne

# The Home

Young ladies, lass, fresh and clean
ripe in pluck of 'morrow's fruit
grabbed, in bite
sweat, swig of ale
and rubbed
'tween teeth and lips
these spring-time maids, fallen
women
sperm and spawn
Each month they grew more
disgraced
six labored layers, stones
waiting down to drop
Their milk soured
in rage and spilt
missing, forgotten months and mouths
shrank, to pitch in dark and dank
femur, hip, pelvis, toe
fetal and fecal
entombed
in unnamed remembrance
The earth refused
to swallow
holding histories hand gloved
The wanted swing and sway, now above
pressing down
in the lightness of laughter
"There's no place like home."

# Voices Heard

She named our cars and coats
our Christmas trees.
Bundled in Ivan - listening for whispering pines.
She knew the call of birds
the song of sea
the saltiness of earth and sky.
She felt weight
which pressed upon her mind
squeezing out voices and thoughts.
The doctor gave her magic pills
to quiet her dreams.
A jacket to hold her secured.
Unable to stretch and touch,
her fingers cold - her nails grew hard.
And when unbound – unwound
a desperate need to pick
the uncoiling.
To let loose the thoughts.
I never told her I hear
the voice of dogs.

# R.D. Taylor

R.D. Taylor is a Florida writer with an extensive career he has published numerous poems, a novel, alleys and even a children's book titled, *The book where Michael meets the Royal Street Elves and learns about Whales, Whale Oil, the Electric Light, and the Two-Headed Sea Serpent.* He ran Poetry on the buses program and Liberty Lunch Poetry Readings in Austin, Tx. He has a BS-Ocean Engineering, Florida Atlantic University, Boca Raton MS-Mechanical/Environmental Engineering, University of Texas, Austin MBA-Pepperdine University, Malibu

http://www.amazon.com/Michael-electric-ostrich-two-headed-serpent/dp/0931604001

# Florida

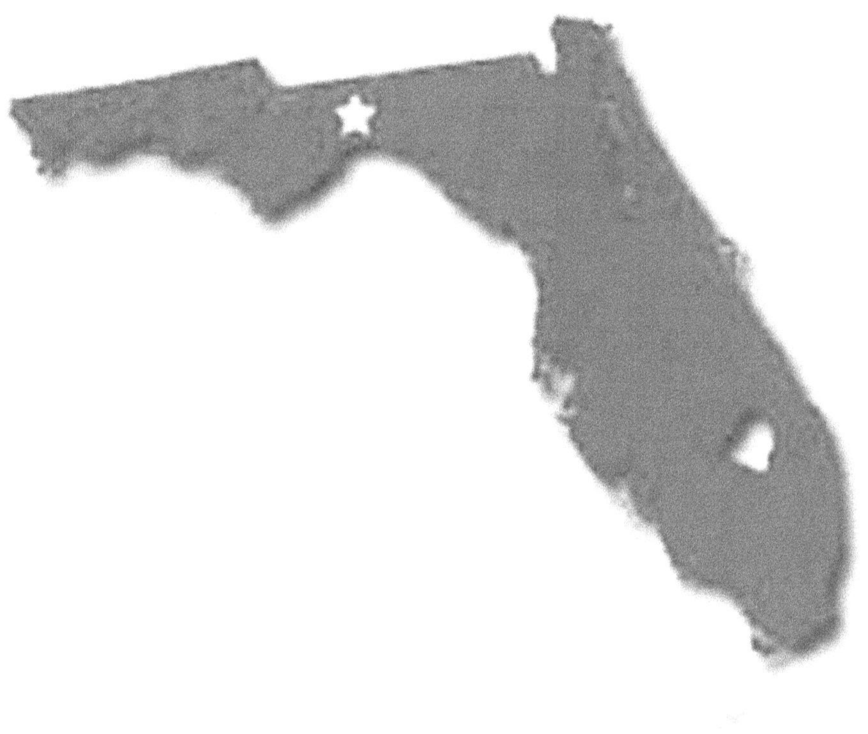

Ron Taylor

# GRAND CANYON

The abyss yawns with a sigh of boredom
So many years waiting for god on the edge of a canyon
The first time was in 1968
Carried by VW German engineering
Puttering across the USA healing
The fractured life of two children of divorce
Who sought solace in mystery
And smoked a joint and joked about hiking
To the bottom of the canyon
I was surprisingly practical and we made love
Then drove to San Francisco
Put flowers in our hair
I lost you somewhere between Marin County
And Austin Texas...we stopped by the canyon together one last time
But didn't talk about going to the bottom
Instead I got educated and grew a suit
And spent thirty years reading about Phantom Ranch
In travel magazines handed out by stewardesses
So many faces I can't remember
Silence in the wisp of wild oats
Bending with the wind
Children come children go
Whispering daddy when you coming home
In a cell phone at 35,000 feet
Suddenly I'm older than social security age
And thank god for one last chance
To correct a lifetime of mistakes
I boarded the plane with my last family
Finished the molly bloom chapter in Ulysses
For the fourth time in the same book I read
Tattered pages and notes in Joyce's handwriting I'd copied
From his manuscript I found at the UT Humanities Research Center
I wanted to do something significant with thirty-eight years of
reading
The work arrogant Professor Ghose had us read in freshman English

Ron Taylor

I intended burying the book somewhere in the Grand Canyon
But we could only carry so much on the mule
I learned god is a mule named Snoopy carrying me
21 miles to the depths of the canyon and back
White as a cloud descending the trail from dust to dust
I did not overcome my fear of heights
But instead embraced the mule while watching its hoofs
Peel away layers of two billion year old earth skin...
I'm not here. My ancestors are not here. Dinosaurs are not here.
What remains?
Devil's backbone...
Devil's switchback...
So much beauty in evil and pain
Your joy is your sorrow comes to my mind again
In the Indian Meadow I as self come undone
The colors hued in stone swirl a temptress' tale
I am two billion years old
Fire and ice...meek and brave...
I have trouble knowing where the canyon wall ends and I begin.
World without end
I without beginning
The stream's white noise explodes my veins
The skies pure blue a musical thought becoming a symphony
I just am...
A grand canyon...hollow...empty...without the need for reason
For a brief moment I don't know if I'm a mule
A shard of granite...a shadowy willow lining a creek bed...
I don't know who I am or what I am as I strive for the bottom of the canyon
Reality is I must reassemble my self
Or I will fall off this damn mule!

Ron Taylor

# SCINTILLATIONS

I've traveled far enough down
this old river dark with pollution,
its only beauty the scintillations
of the moonlight reflecting from its waters
like fireflies escaping from a jar.
I grab at those fireflies...
They've been with me long enough I think they're mine.
They escape, glad to be free
like sparks stinging the water
and turning ugliness into beauty.
I've known a few scintillations.
They are brief flares
screaming across the night sky...
Once I sat alone at the picnic in '71
(ten years after Roger Maris broke the Babe's record)
I clutched the Most Valuable Player award
feeling every eye on me whether they liked it or not.
They say Roger Maris felt that way.
It was the day I first heard you speak.
Your voice sounded happy
and the hotdogs were delicious.
The colors of the clothing you wore that day
Were like a garland for my eyes.
I didn't know you'd become my best friend.
For some reason
I liked watching your butt when we climbed trees together.
And your smile as if you were so much older and wiser than me.
I eventually understood.
Years later we rode the Staten Island ferry
and I couldn't tell the stars from the Manhattan skyline.
They danced about you
like the eyes from a thousand generations watching.
And the time in the Colorado Mountains
where the evergreen branches bent low,
weighed like snow shovels full of snow.
The snow fell warm and light

as we buried ourselves in the snowdrift
Pretending we lived in an igloo
we were just crazy enough to lose our clothes
and counted the rainbows in each unique snowflake.
Your body glowed sweetly red as a plum against the white.
The last time I saw you
the Pacific Ocean couldn't hold
your thin and pliant body
in its kelp bed,
clear as crystal and green as emeralds.
You exploded from the water
like a shark with black hair beaching itself
and collapsed on top of me.
I drowned in the sand
and your mouth was salty like the sea...
your face burnt a hole in the sky.
Now I spend my days counting clouds
hurting to see you again.
There seems an endless number of clouds.
And in the night...
I try until my mind bursts
wishing fireflies back into a jar.

Ron Taylor

# An Arrow to God

A medieval monk
Labored in meditation in a cloistered room
Desperate for union he imagined
An arrow of love to pierce the heart of god
Sleek, long and steadied by a feather
The smooth shaft and lethal point
Arches elegant to the heart of the sixteen year old boy
Frozen by fear that binds all in the last moment
Such a metaphor is the arrow
Is it the simple, natural beauty of its honed wood?
Or the finality of its business end
That intrigues one?
Was the arch of the arrow a symbol of the monk's life?
The solid shaft an enduring, unrequited love
The impacted fatal triangle
The terminus one shares with god?
In today's imagery would it be a rocket to the moon
Or the rocket propelled grenade
The monk would use to make his point
That All we need is love....
Perhaps the monk should ask John Lennon
Or just leave the confines of his room
Grab a handful of moist earth
Smell it
And look at the cerulean sky
The mongrel dog might catch his eye
And in fear he may return to his room
Not seeing the connection
Between the earth, the sky, that dog and himself
He only sees the differences
Justifies separation of body and soul
And wonders
Why god doesn't speak to him
All we need is love....
And the wisdom of silence...and science!

# United Kingdom

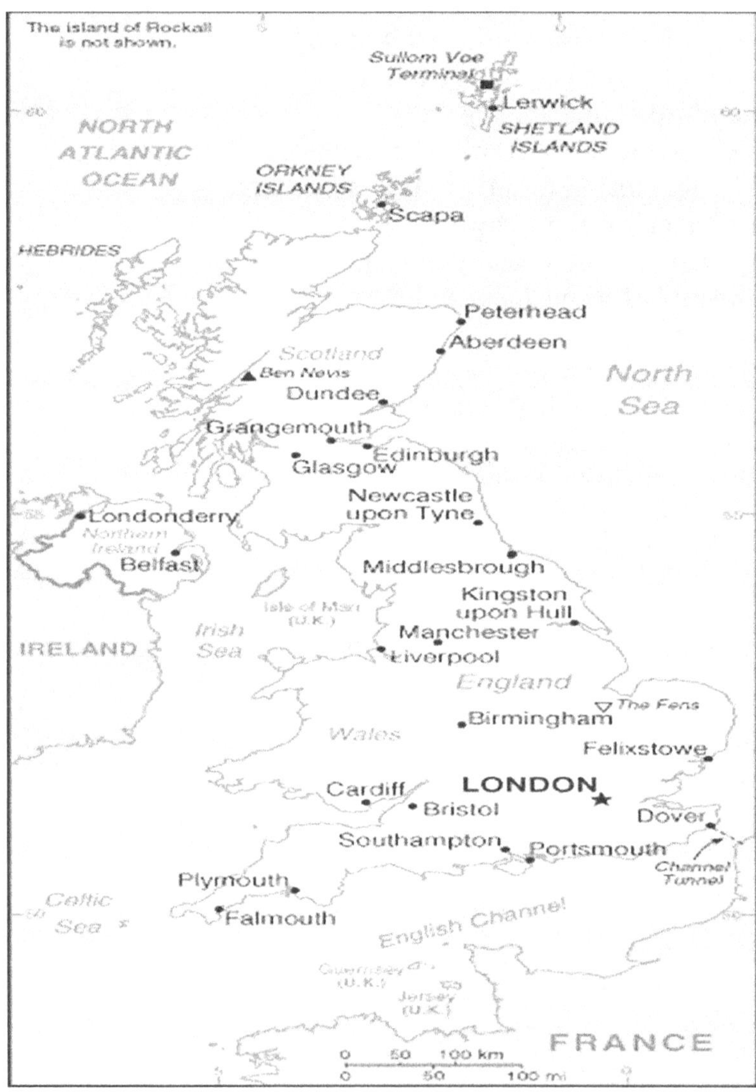

# Martin David Edwards

Martin David Edwards lives in London, UK. He likes to write stories with quirky characters and themes. His work has previously been published in Psychopomp, Bento Box, the Metric, Streetcake, Storyboard, Winamop, and Sein und Werden magazines, and in the anthology "Allusions of Innocence" by Solarwyrm Press. Martin is also a photographer and has exhibited his work in shows in London and New York. His web site is

www.storiesbymartin.com.

Martin David Edwards

martin@storiesbymartin.com

# The Waterfall

## By:

## Martin David Edwards

Eirwin tugs at her bonnet then covers her neck with her hand. A jolt from the track prompts her to turn around to Derwen, holding the reigns of the horse in his outstretched hands. He stares ahead, his blue eyes burning a path through the trees like crystals. In the distance, they can hear water drumming like a sheet of sound.

"I wanted the flowers," she says.

Derwen tightens the reins in response, his knuckles turning white.

"The wedding," she continues. "For tomorrow, while the scents are still fresh."

As the cart swerves through a puddle, he clucks at the horse. Eirwin's mother had frowned in the kitchen at the request; her hand paused in a bowl of dough. There were the wedding preparations to be finished and her sister would be arriving later with a baby to feed. However, Eirwin had replied that she needed the air. Her mother had nodded, a fleck of dough dropping from her fingertips. She could take Derwen in the cart and was to be back before her sister came.

Derwen is still having his doubts; Eirwin is sure from his eyes fixed ahead. She had insisted on the waterfall, turning right outside the farm when they should have turned left for the village. A hired hand, her father called him; Derwen would not contradict her, the second and final daughter to be married. But not a servant.

The drumming from the waterfall grows louder, pulsing through her veins. She can feel her body beginning to tingle, her heartbeat quickening. With a neigh from the horse, the cart slows to a halt.

Derwen steps off and holds out his hand to steady Eirwin. They touch fleetingly as she adjusts her dress. His skin is streaked with the brown earth of the farm, its roughness grating her own. He must have been ploughing in the morning, she thinks. Eirwin inspects her dress of white lace, her arms bare. It was an early wedding present from her sister. She swallows hard, feeling guilty at what must happen next.

Half following her down the path to the waterfall, Derwen returns to the cart when she maintains her pace instead of slowing for him. From the corner of her eye, she sees him sit on the front bench of the cart and gaze at the surrounding hills, already lost. She follows the path downward through the rocks, taking care not to slip. Pausing with her arms held out for balance, she breathes in the mist from the water and prepares herself.

The crank of a wheel shaft interrupts her. Alongside the farm's cart a carriage has appeared, its paintwork gilded in silver. A footman in red livery opens its door and a family clatters out, two children chattering and jumping away. For a moment, Eirwin wonders if Derwen will be jealous of the footman, but he is focused on his private reverie.

Eirwin waits to be sure that the family have not changed their mind then checks the path. She is still alone. Craning her neck, she follows the stream of water cascading through the rocks above her, a thin line of white blurring through the greenness of the moss. She is reminded of milk, but shakes her bonnet and carries on navigating between the glistening rocks. Future brides, her mother said, are not supposed to think too much.

A brilliant yellow flash catches her eye from the side of the path and she sees a buttercup fluttering in the breeze from the waterfall.

Eirwin lets the petals glide through her fingers like silk and leaves the flower unpicked.

"Most suitable as a match," her parents had announced six months ago. Thomas was a future husband with prospects, due to inherit a farm in the next valley with three times the number of sheep. "At twenty, you're at the best years of your life," her mother added, looking down at her feet. Only the date was to be decided, in case Thomas might change his mind.

Thomas. Eirwin's hand rises to her neck again. She shudders and breathes in the mist to try to calm herself. His age could be understood; a gap of a decade was common and his farm had five versions of Derwen. Moreover, she could not remain at home, becoming a spinster while her nieces and nephews grew.

She touches her neck for a third time. Her lips form his name but leave the letters unfinished. Thomas has taken her a walk during their brief courtship, the engagement ring barely ordered. She could smell the sweetness of whisky on his breath as he had leaned over to kiss her and had turned her face instinctively away. A warm saltiness shocked her. Thomas had licked her neck. Until their wedding night, he had murmured in her ear. She would be worth the wait.

"Eirwin," she hears and wonders if Derwen is calling her name, reminding her to return to the farm in time for her sister. Only the rocks of the path are behind her. She lets her eyes roam over the waterfall and sways. The water must be speaking to her. As a child, she was always prone to dreaming.

Reversing her direction, she skips through the rocks and checks to the side of the waterfall, straining on tiptoe. The slops of the surrounding hills appear covered in Christmas trees. She never took the route to the top when she and her sister had come as children, seeing only innocence ahead.

Eirwin's feet jar on boulders as she scrambles up the hill. A droplet of water splashes on her bare arms, but she feels no need to shiver or warm herself. She catches a glimpse of the meadow beyond the waterfall as a branch swings and ducks, not wanting to be seen by the family picnicking or by Derwen either.

At the top of the hill, her lips widen into a smile and then a frown crosses her face, the beginnings of her mother. Touching her neck, she still remembers the salty touch. There is no reason she can give for a refusal at the altar, no secret love, no longing for anywhere else except where she has come to be.

The water grows into a roar as she steps closer to the edge of the rocks. Eirwin looks down and sees the waterfall running through the grey granite. The farm's cart and the carriage sparkle through the trees. She can just make out the bare plank of the cart's front seat; perhaps Derwen has gone to pick the flowers on her behalf, tired of waiting.

She takes off her shoes, muddy and ruined from the climb. Her mother will be furious. Placing them by a fern with their heels lined up, she dips her toes into the water. She is expecting to gasp, but the water caresses her feet as she dreams a lover would.

"We'll be late for your sister," a voice shouts over the water. Derwen is standing at the pool by the bottom of the waterfall, scratching his head with his dirt-encrusted hands. There are no flowers drooping from inside his palms.

Eirwin releases the tie holding her bonnet in place and shakes her hair loose in cascades of cola-like black.

"I'll get you down. You shouldn't have gone climbing on your own. Your father," Derwen calls, his throat tightening. His voice trails away to be replaced by the taps of pebbles bouncing down the path. As he climbs, she stretches her feet and the water laps at her ankles.

"There is always a way. We could go together," Derwen pleads besides her, panting from his rapid climb. Leaning forward, he is ready to catch her like an improbable leopard.

Eirwin rocks on her toes, her dress billowing around her. Derwen drops his arms, but she does not come to him. He blushes scarlet and wipes a line of earth across his mouth, trying to undo his words. Then she smiles at him, edges further into the flowing water and disappears.

With a shout, Derwen darts to the rock cliff. His hand slips when he tries to look down, dreading what he will see next.

However, as he scans the rocks, only the shimmer of the moss greets him. In the pool at the waterfall's base, there is neither floating white dress nor hair weaving below the surface like reeds.

No gash of blood stains the rocks with a wetness familiar from the farm. Cupping his eyes, he even checks the meadow before his shoulders slump.

The bubbling of the waterfall echoes in his head as he wonders if he is hallucinating. No one could possibly believe him. The parents will declare him mad, a conjurer, a murderer who makes his bodies disappear.

A babble of children's voices floats across the water. The family is returning to the coach, the footman is holding the door open and standing to attention.

Cardiff, Derwen decides. He will say that Eirwin escaped from him and tricked a ride in the carriage, the footman her accomplice. From the city, she could travel anywhere before they could check. However, at the waterfall, she will always be his.

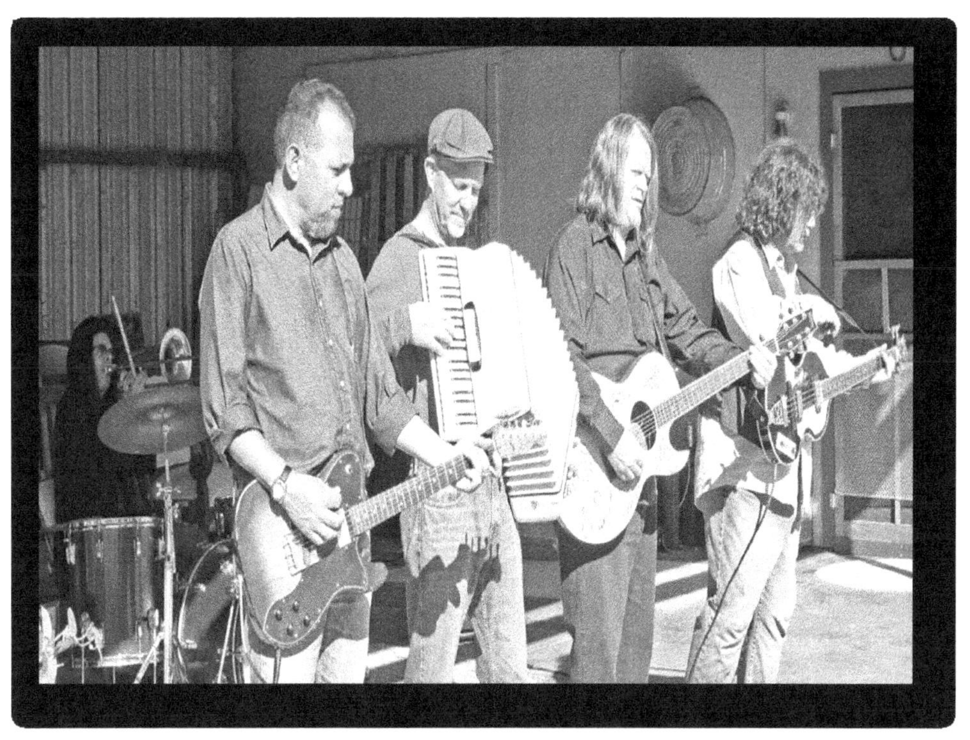

# MILAGRO SAINTS

Current Lineup:

**SD Ineson:Vocals, Acoustic Rhythm Guitar Lee Kirby: Hammond Organ, Piano, Harmonica, Melodica Roberto Morales: Electric guitar/mandolin Smitty:Lap Steel Steve Samosky:Bass Jick wins-Low: vocals, drums, bass, trombone, guitars, fiddle**

Milagro Saints are a Raleigh NC based "Poetic Roots Rock Americana" band that has been busy touring for the past few years promoting their albums. They recorded a six song EP the "Mighty Road Songs" in 2013 to celebrate their continuing participation in the Woody Guthrie Folk Festival. That fell right on the heels of their 2012 album "Chance and Circumstance" (Moon Caravan Records).

Both releases achieved national radio play at AAA in the US (charting on Roots Music Radio Folk/Roots chart) and on charting stations in France, Belgium, Denmark, Sweden, Germany, The U.K. and The Netherlands.

The band originally formed in NYC around the songwriting, singing and acoustic guitar of Englishman SD Ineson, keyboardist Lee Kirby and singer/multi-instrumentalist Joyce Bowden but moved to North Carolina when they were signed to indy label MoodFood, (which had released the debut album by Ryan Adams' Whiskeytown, one of the originators of the "alt.country" genre).

They opened for 10,000 Maniacs at the Lowell MA Summer Music Series for the 50th anniversary of Jack Kerouac's book "On the Road" and Shakori Hills Festival alongside band such as Carolina Chocolate Drops.

To support radio play the band had been touring the East Coast and Mid-West playing an endless list of live radio sessions. Now they have been back in North Carolina for a little while and in between shows have been working on their new album, **"TUPELO"** which will come out this spring.

"One of the earliest bands I reviewed for Country Music News International was Milagro Saints. They were probably the reason why I kept on writing reviews. Stephen David Ineson is the singer, songwriter, and acoustic rhythm guitar player. I've known a great deal of people on the many travels throughout my life. So far, in doing this I've made a great deal more acquaintances that I feel rather blessed to be able to get to know. For an active, touring and recording band you wouldn't expect that any of the members would have time to get in touch with you personally for liking their Facebook page.

With Milagro Saints it was a lot different though. I was setting up a new page because I wanted to separate music from short story writers, reviewers, poetry groups, and publishing houses. I went into that page and liked theirs. The new page I was setting up had a name completely different than my own. Not even a day later, I received a, thanks, from Stephen himself. Just from my different pages I know how hard it is to keep up with this, and I am stuck at my house. I'm not out selling books like I should be, and I'm definitely not performing.

We communicated back and forth a bit and I explained that I wrote a review about them (as well as, apologized for it because it was one of the first reviews I did). Anyway, I asked if it'd be alright if I asked him a few questions for a short interview. To my surprise he agreed so I prepared my five questions. Here's what I asked:

**Question** – I came across your band while writing reviews for a Country Music News International. Everything I've read about Milagro Saints seems to place you in a different category; Americana Rock, Rugged Folk, Roots, Jam Band, etc.etc. I hate to ask, but if you had to categorize your music what genre do you believe it would fit with?
**Stephen** - Americana Roots Rock is our usual genre, although that's big and wide selection of music.
**Question** – On *Chances and Circumstances,* I've seen a great deal about "These Things about You." My favorite song if I had to choose one is, "Pennsylvania Rose." Which song and from what album is your least favorite song to perform, due to the emotional meaning behind the writing.

**Stephen** - I like to perform my most personally emotional songs! PA Rose is directly about my wife her Irish family history- our fans like it too because it's so upfront and often my wife is in the audience.
**Question -** You probably always get asked this question, but do you first write the lyrics, or do you first come up with the melody on guitar and the lyrics follow?
**Stephen -** Regarding songwriting, huh I usually get what I think is a good tune and then add lyrics.
**Question –** The differences between playing in bars and clubs vs. playing at outdoor festivals are enormous. Which do you prefer more?
**Stephen -** I think I prefer outdoor venues. bars are ok but usually they're a late night.
**Question-** Every band seems to have a story behind their name, how did you guys come up with the name Milagro Saints, and what is the meaning behind it?
**Stephen** – The band name evolved from the concept of Milagros being those Mexican religious talismans, it combines art and spirituality which I think music and songs also do that. I had a dream that said call the band Milagro Saints- John Lennon said he had a similar dream visitation- something about a flaming pie and beetles with an 'a'.

After answering my questions, he even went one further and told me of the upcoming shows they had coming, and told me to send him a message and he'd hook it up where we could meet up at the show. I already missed those shows but hopefully they'll be playing a Florida outdoor soon. They're in North Carolina so that's not unimaginable. Also, for anyone over in Europe keep an eye out for them because I read on their site that they have been getting airplay over there. Personally, I'm hoping I can get them in the next issue of my CoffeeShop Blues Literary Journal we are working on now.

**Jeremy Frost for Country Music News International"**

Well, SD Ineson sent me the photo for the front of this section and the MP3 for the title track of the new album. He was more than happy to oblige and he is the type of guy, scratch that…They are that kind of band which I should have expected no less from. The new album, "**TUPELO**" will be coming out this spring 2015. If you want to get a taste of what they sound like just go to their website. There is a continuous player there for anyone to listen to.

**CHECK OUT the Milagro Saints social media world**

**Twitter:** twitter.com/milagrosaints

**Facebook:** Facebook.com/milagrosaints

**WRITE A LETTER or EMAIL** mooncaravan@yahoo.com
**Moon Caravan Records HQ**
**511 Florence St. Raleigh NC 27603**

**Website : http://www.milagrosaints.com/**
**Reverbnation: http://www.reverbnation.com/msaints**
**Sonicbids: http://www.sonicbids.com/band/milagrosaints2/audio/**
**Bandcamp: http://milagrosaints.bandcamp.com/**

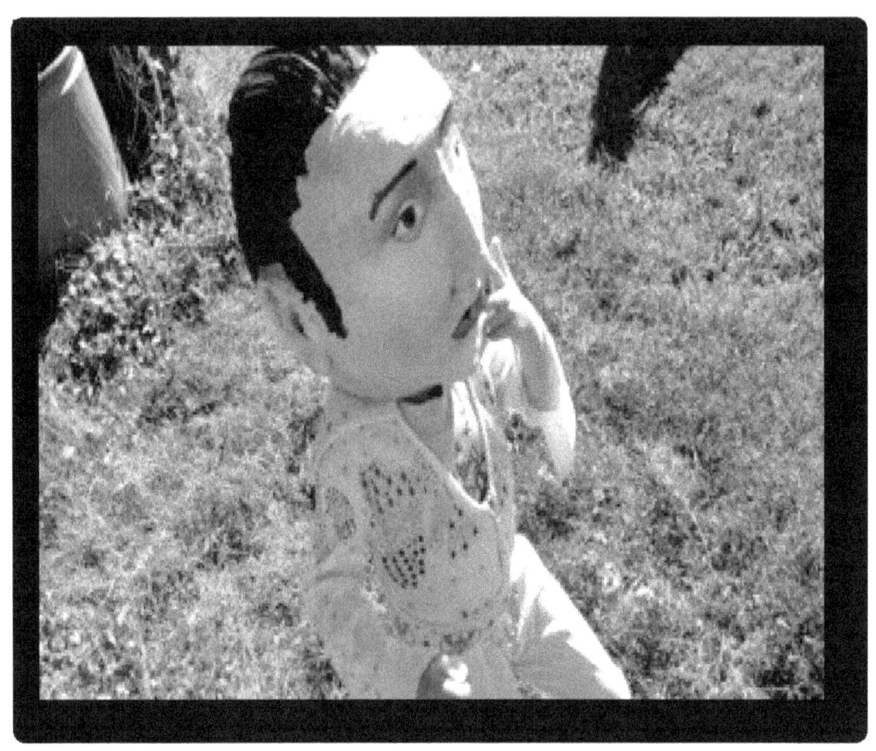

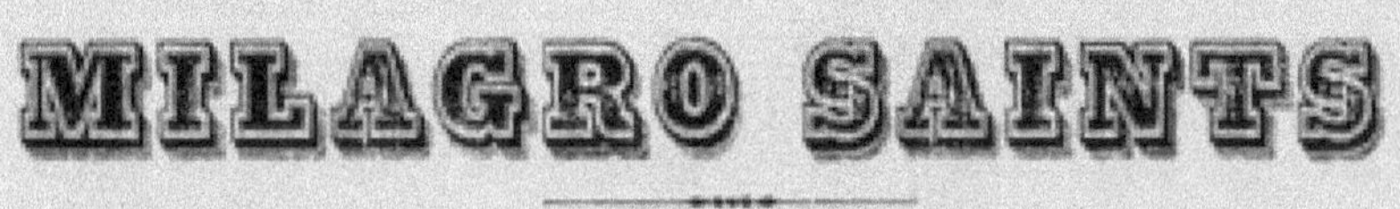


**The new album TUPELO will be out later in the spring of 2015. If you click the picture above it should bring you to the new video for the title track. If you have a print version of this, the Youtube link is:**

http://youtu.be/k_tB3Hzp5Ck

# TUPELO

PLEASE TO MEET YOU, TAKE MY HAND,

AND LET'S GO TO TUPELO
LET'S TAKE SOME TIME ON A HIGHWAY DRIVE,
A FEW MILES, TAKE IT SLOW

SEND ME A MESSAGE ON THE TELEGRAPH WIRE, &
TELL ME,

"YES OR NO"
MY HEART IS FROZEN IN SPACE AND TIME,
TIL I KNOW, WHAT YOU KNOW, ABOUT TU-PE-LO

I HEARD A WHISPER FROM A FRIEND OF MINE
THINK YOU KNOW… MISTER STONE?
HE SAID YOU MET A STRANGER FROM OUT OF TOWN
AND HE TOLD YOU WHAT ?... I DON'T KNOW

CALL ME LATER ON THE TELEPHONE LINE &
WHISPER,
"YES OR NO"

MY MIND IS FOGGY AND MY FEET ARE ON FIRE
TIL I KNOW, WHAT YOU KNOW, ABOUT TU-PE-LO

TORNADO IN TUPELO IN 1936 OR SO
PUT ELVIS AND HIS TWIN IN A SPIN AND HEAVEN
KNOWS
THE NATCHEZ TRACE AND THE CHICKASAW
SAVED THEIR SOULS- AND BLESSED THEIR BONES
TORNADO IN TUPELO IN 19 - 36 OR SO

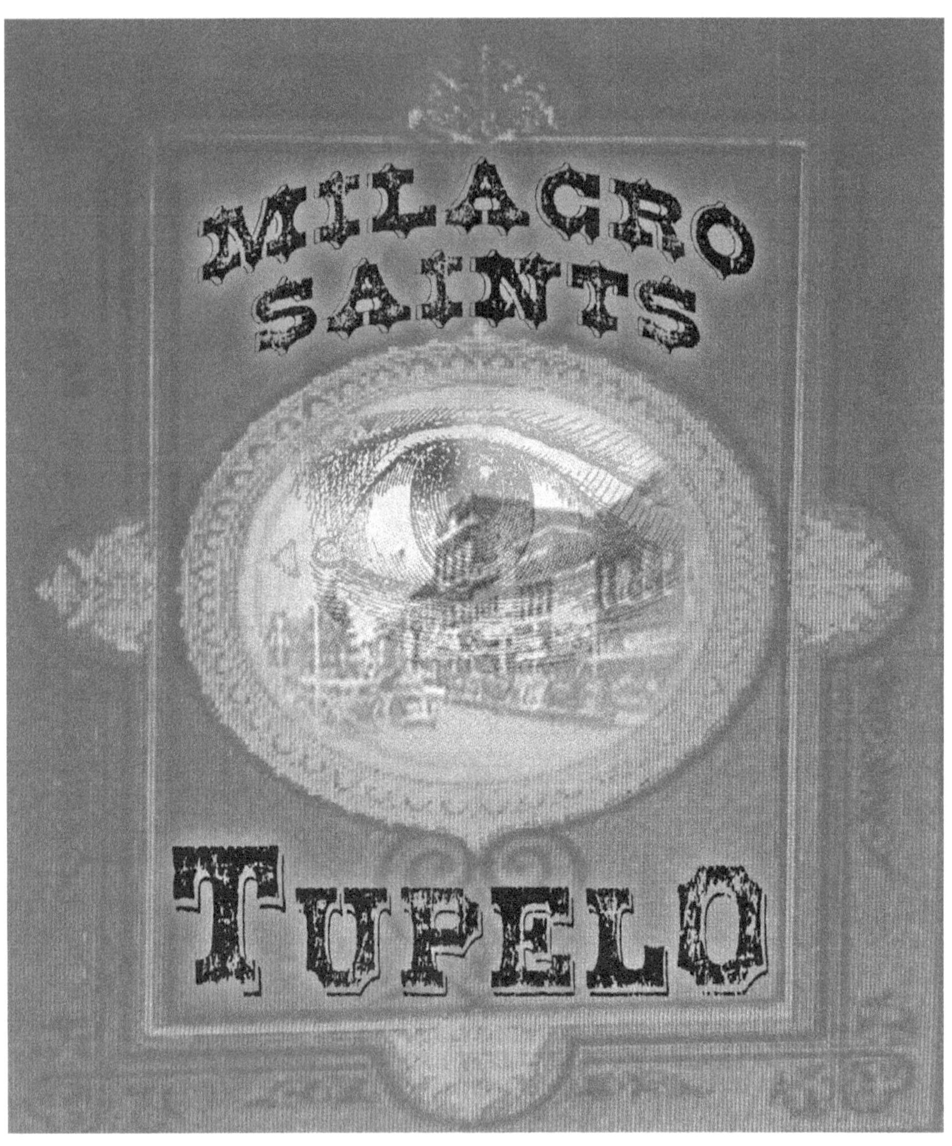
MILAGRO
SAINTS
TUPELO

# Texas

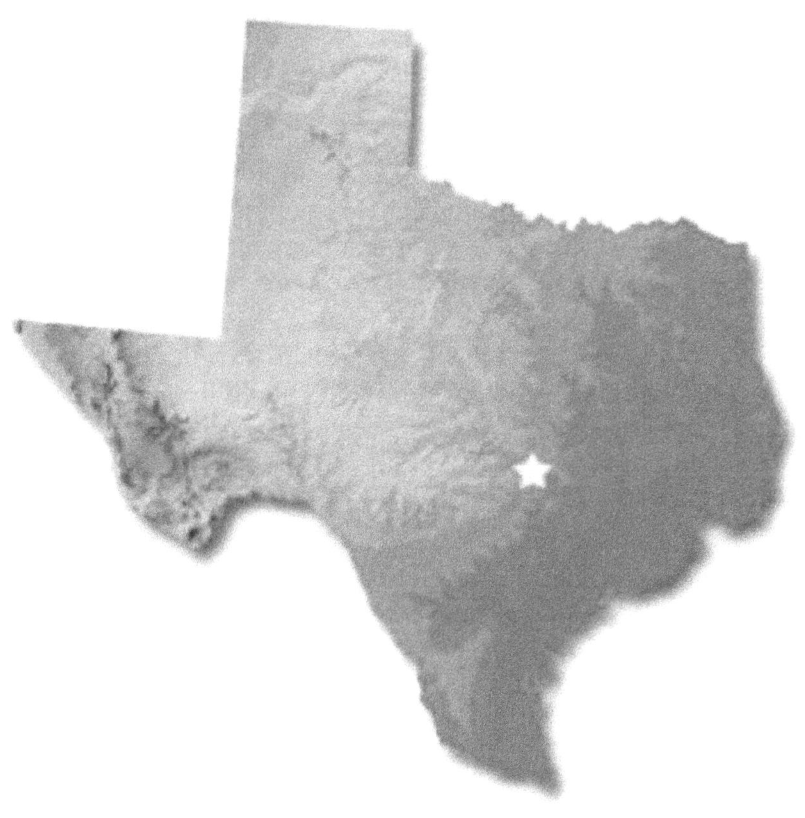

# Apple Gidley

A transient life has seen Apple Gidley live in countries as diverse as Papua New Guinea and Thailand, or Equatorial Guinea and the USA, and another eight in between. Her memoir, Expat Life Slice by Slice, tells of the highs and lows of that nomadic life - one she wouldn't trade for all the proverbial tea in one of the places she hasn't lived, China. Her travel articles are filled with colour, and spiced with subtleties that take the arm-chair-traveller to that country, or make the experienced traveller add it to their list. She draws on her experiences for her pieces on expatriate living, which offer down-to-earth observations and encouragement to those about to embark on the trail, or who already live the life.

Gidley writes a regular blog at my.telegraph.co.uk/applegidley and is currently working on her second novel, and a book of short stories. www.applegidley.com

# SEEING RED

**By:**

## Apple Gidley

Peering out into the shadowy promise of day Gemma shuddered as the wind snapped the tent flap from her grasp, the canvas flapping wildly.

Shrugging a khaki shirt over the cami she'd slept in, she knew it wouldn't take long for the sweat to start its inexorable slide down between her breasts to pool in a soggy mess at the waistband of her shorts. It still surprised her that the thick socks she tugged on each day actually lived up to their promise of keeping her feet cool and dry. Tipping her ankle boots upside down, she shook them hard listening for the slither of scorpion hitting the sandy groundsheet. It was difficult to see in the dim glow of the hurricane lamp but feeling confident she wriggled her toes into the boots and tied them tightly. Gemma ripped the duct tape off the zipper track of her holdall. The zip had been no match for the heat and humidity and had jammed within days of her arrival. Her fingers probed for the disc shaped tin of Tiger Balm; bug prevention she was convinced worked. Refilling her backpack with the day's essentials she remembered to toss in another tub of talc: the gloves provided stuck to her fingers making them itchy and sore.

Ready, she said to the photo jammed under the rim of the 6x4 inch mirror she'd tossed into her luggage at the last moment, the thought of raggedy eyebrows too much even for her rare vanity. The photo booth shot was tattered and she smiled as she smoothed the exposed edges thinking of the afternoon it had been taken in Grand Central Station.

A soft clinking told her Ahmed was already in the mess tent, the smell of coffee blowing with the sand as she unbuckled the fly flap and faced the day. What she wouldn't give for one of her father's blueberry pancakes right now she thought as stepping over guy ropes she ducked into the tent to find Simon seated at the trestle table, mulishly eyeing his tin mug.

"Good morning Sim," she said sliding along the bench opposite. "You look pissed already, what's up?"

"Bloody genny's down again. Raja's working on her now. No point collecting otherwise. Shit I hate this place," he said, and thumping his mug down glanced up at Gemma. "How come you look clean and well rested after a night like that?"

"Good dreams," she grinned. "If you hate it so much why do you keep coming back?" she asked the prematurely wrinkled face across the plank table.

"Someone has to," he muttered. "Hey Ahmed, any more of the black stuff my friend, before we start another hellish day?"

Gemma watched as Ahmed shuffled over with a battered tin pot of freshly brewed coffee, his bare feet tracing their passage across the sand.

"Salam Ahmed," she greeted the wizened man in his grey jelaba, darker at the hem where grime had become part of the fabric.

"Sabah el kheer, Dokor Gemma," he replied, his words whistling through the gaps in his teeth, gums exposed in a vivid pink slash.

"Boss," he said to Sim, "Raja he say me bloody genny be fix soon soon."

Gemma smiled into the sweet black coffee. The shock at the free use of swearing amongst all the crew had initially rankled but she had soon found herself aping their speech. It was the first time she had worked with Brits and she found the easy humour in grim moments a surprising stress reliever.

"I don't know how I'll manage with bagels, and butter, and jam when I get home," she said as she bit into the dry saltines that were their staple breakfast fare.

"Yeah, well don't get too fond of those luv," Sim said nodding to the packet on the table, "if the supply truck doesn't get through soon they'll be rationed too," and draining his coffee stood up. "Come on, let's get cracking! Get as many through the doors before the sun gets too high, otherwise we'll have 'em fainting left, right an' bloody centre."

Gemma spluttered as the dregs hit the back of her throat. "Ugh," she said following Sim into the blooming dawn, spitting coffee grounds into her hands before wiping them on her shorts and reaching for the hand sanitizer clipped at her waist.

Threading their way to the main tent identified by the Red Cross flag, they dodged meagre awnings sheltering listless women and grizzling infants. Some of the older, stronger children were nursing precious containers filled with a few inches of water as they returned from the tank, fiercely presided over by Martin, a Sudanese of immense proportions and a prodigious memory. Educated in Baltimore, he was the camp Scrabble champion.

"Bloody hell, look at them Gemma," Sim said, nodding at the line of scrawny men and women as they neared the dispensary tent. "They have nothing and yet here they are lining up to give what they do have. Some of the lazy bastards back home should see this." Gemma nodded as they ducked into the large tent, open on two sides since the main genny died, and walked to the tables at the back. The lack of air had won over a more sterile environment.

"Are we ready for this?" Gemma asked the aides preparing syringes, their uniforms of cargo shorts and cheerful Tees, a splash of colour amidst the misery of ochre. "Okay, let's do it. A blood drive, Sudanese-style."

Warning shouts came from the queue outside, followed by panicked screams that reverberated along the rows of canvas, then the gunfire. The rebels were back. Gemma's thoughts flew to the photo as, grabbing a white cloth to show their status, she ran towards the mayhem.

# Italy

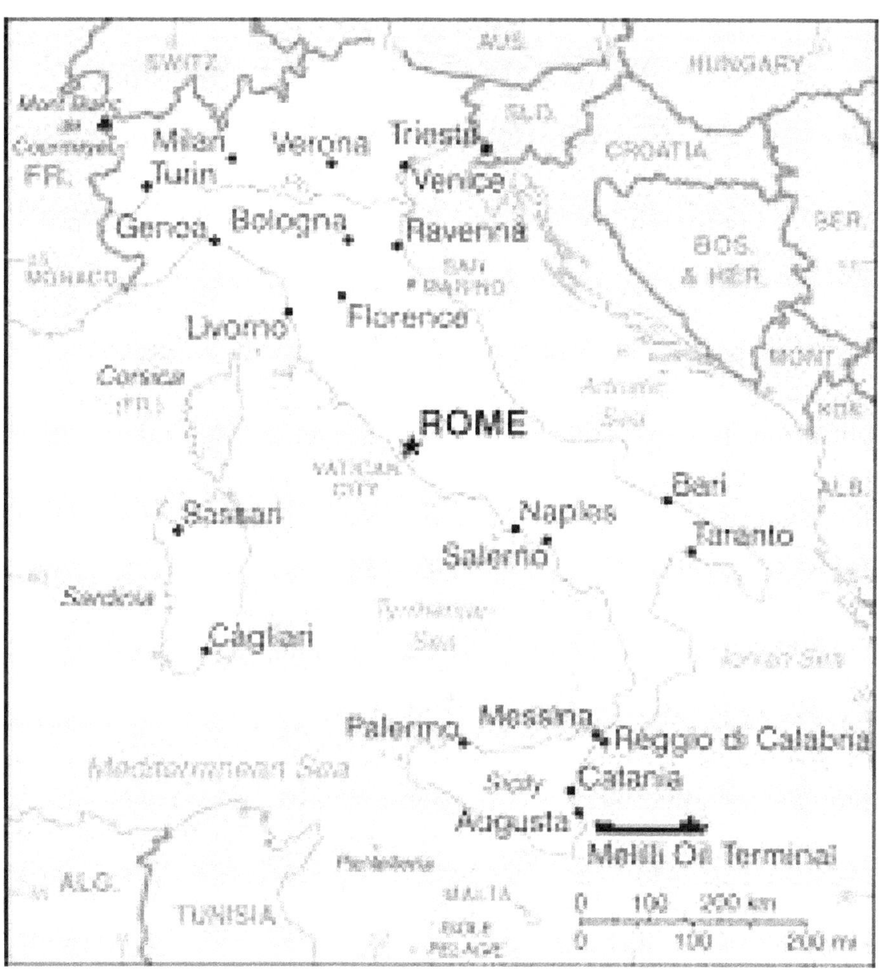

SWITZ.
AUS.
HUNGARY
FR.
Milan
Turin
Verona
Trieste
Venice
SLO.
CROATIA
Genoa
Bologna
Ravenna
BOS. & HER.
SER.
MONACO
SAN MARINO
Livorno
Florence
Corsica (FR.)
MONT.
ROME
VATICAN CITY
Bari
ALB.
Sassari
Naples
Taranto
Salerno
Sardinia
Cagliari
Palermo
Messina
Reggio di Calabria
Sicily
Catania
Augusta
Melilli Oil Terminal
ALG.
TUNISIA
MALTA
0 100 200 km
0 100 200 mi

# Janet Butler

Janet Butler lives in Victorian Alameda with Fulmi, a lovely Spaniel mix she rescued in Italy and brought back with her to the states. She began both writing and painting during her 20 years in central Italy. In Alameda she is moderator of a monthly meetup for local literati, Poetry and Prose at the Blue Danube Coffee Shop. As watercolor painter, belongs to the Frank Bette Art Center, and recently had five drawings selected for show in a month long exhibit of the Tuesday night figure drawing class. Her most recent chapbook, "Upheaval", was one of three winners in the Red Ochre Press Chapbook Contest for 2012, and 10 tanka will be published in an upcoming issue of Undertow.

Her watercolors and drawings may be viewed at:

http://janet-butler.fineartamerica.com.

http://www.angelfire.com/ar/watercolors2

Watercolors & Poetry
http://janet-butler.fineartamerica.com

Amazon.com: poetry by Janet Butler
5 poetry collections for Kindle

Janet Butler

# Morning, Rome

I stretch and breathe in morning.
It fills me with coolness
a primal moment.

The city below me
shifts -
its pieces

a slow dance,
the random pattern of
a disjointed minuet.

The white light of an 8 am sun
cleans streets, the acrid scent
of traffic

not unpleasant.
Conversations float up,
invite me in

their lush plump vowels
ripe fruit
falling at my feet.

Janet Butler

# Plein air Sunday

I walk into Sunday's garden, barefooted,
weekday's grime left at the gate.

The morning is sweet with the coolness
of night, puddles in shadows seeping deep

into brown-black earth, van dyke browns,
rich with an undertone of red

color my brush dips into,
the afternoon a canvas I dream on.

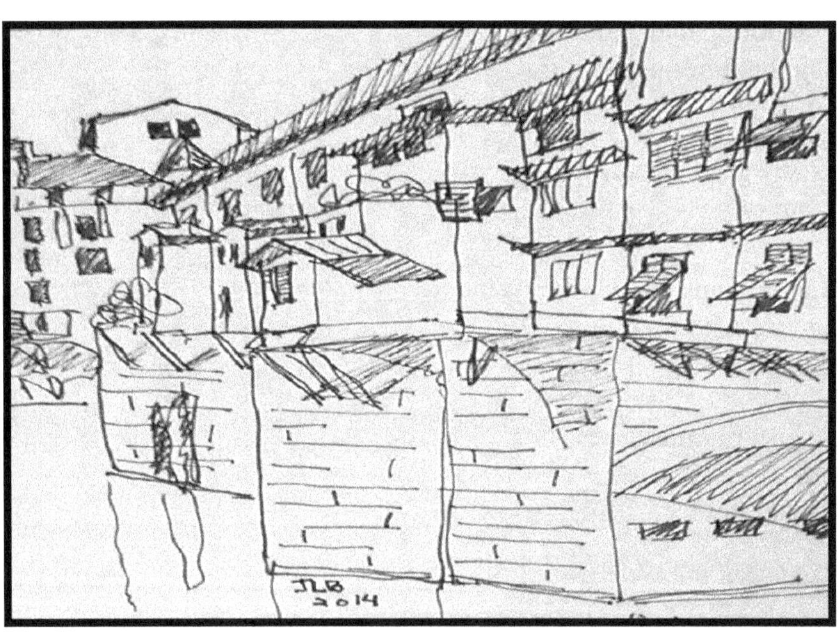


**Ponte Vecchio, Florence, Italy**
http://fineartamerica.com/featured/ponte-vecchio-in-florence-janet-butler.html

Janet Butler

# Evening walk

The Indian Summer hours are warm,
the blowsy heat of full-breasted earth.

Star dust from those bobbles
strung across night shimmers on your lips.
Street lights observe us as we walk,
soft eyes lowered, discrete.

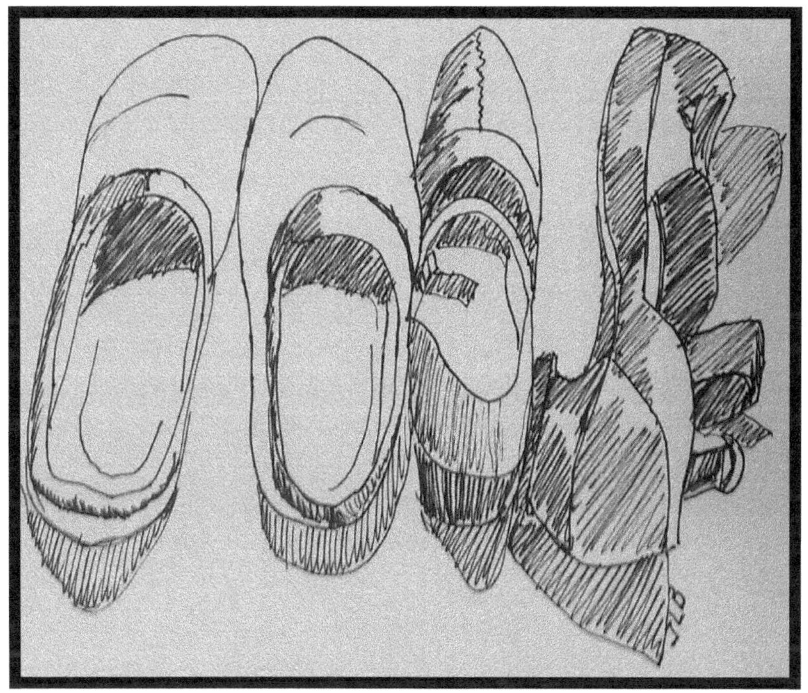

**Slippers and Shoes**

**http://fineartamerica.com/featured/1-kickstarter-reward-4-2-5-janet-butler.html**

Janet Butler

# Hibiscus

I open a window and a bouquet of early evening
drifts in,
the shrill screams of happy kids
faking fear as they run and coyly fall
on summer grass,
soft,
scented with the spice of a
hot July day like their warm,
brown-skinned mothers,
eyes soft and deep as the southern nights
they left. They sing the music of those faraway lands
in fat-voweled words,
all cadence and rhythm,
they dim their reds and greens
to the subtle shades of northern lights,
gather their children close in arms that smell of sun and flowers,
rich
like the earth they blossomed from.

Janet Butler

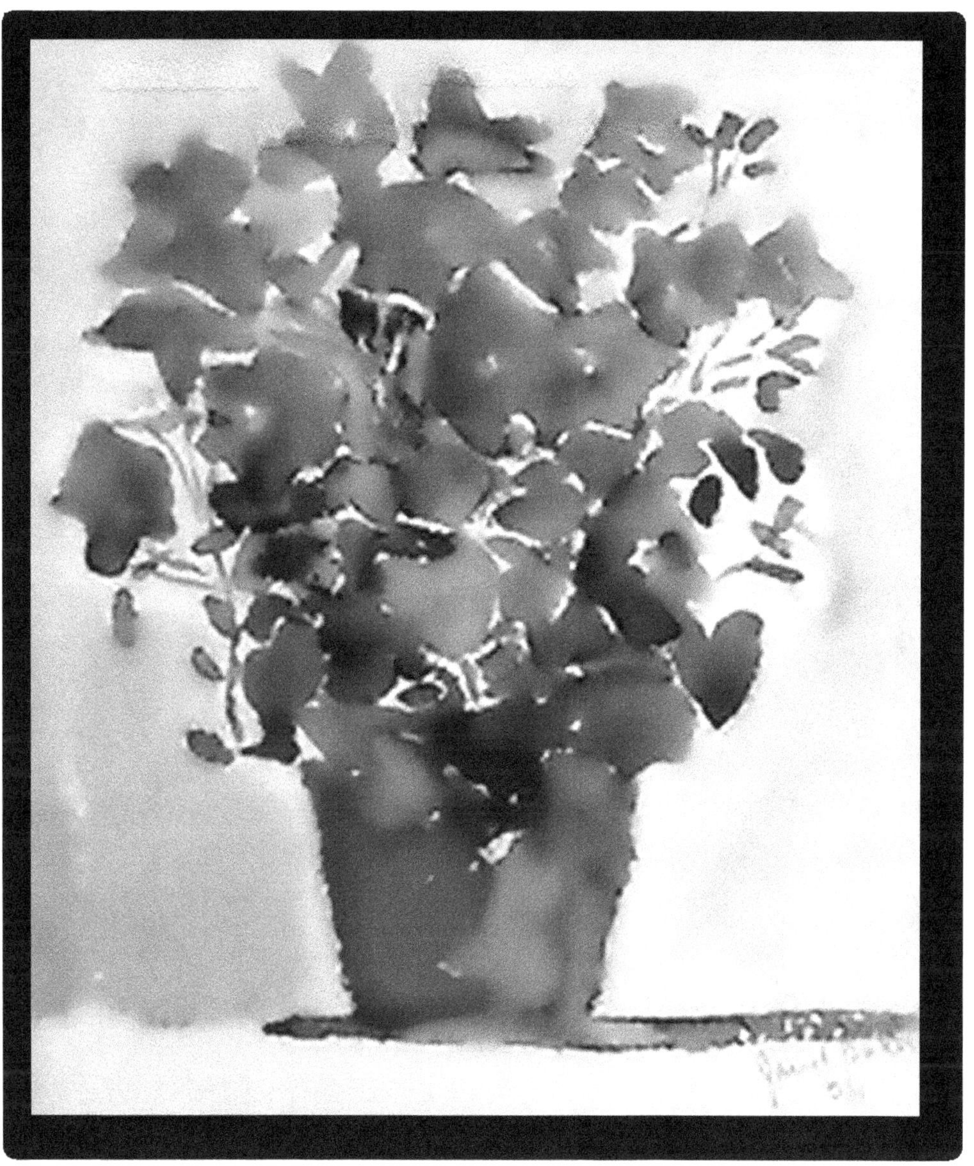

**Bluebells**

**http://fineartamerica.com/featured/bluebells-janet-butler.html**

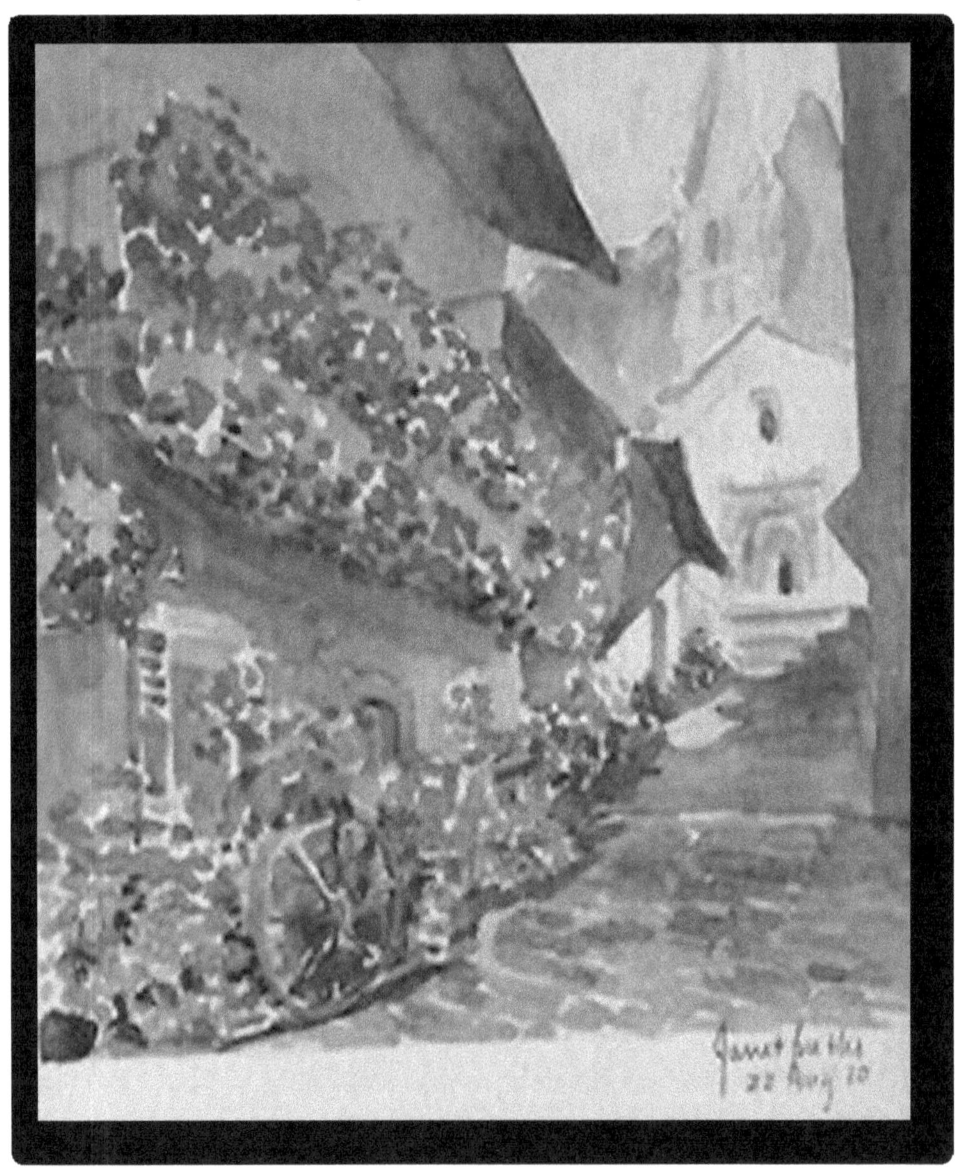


**Sunday Morning Northern Italy**

**http://fineartamerica.com/featured/sunday-morning-northern-italy-janet-butler.html**

Janet Butler

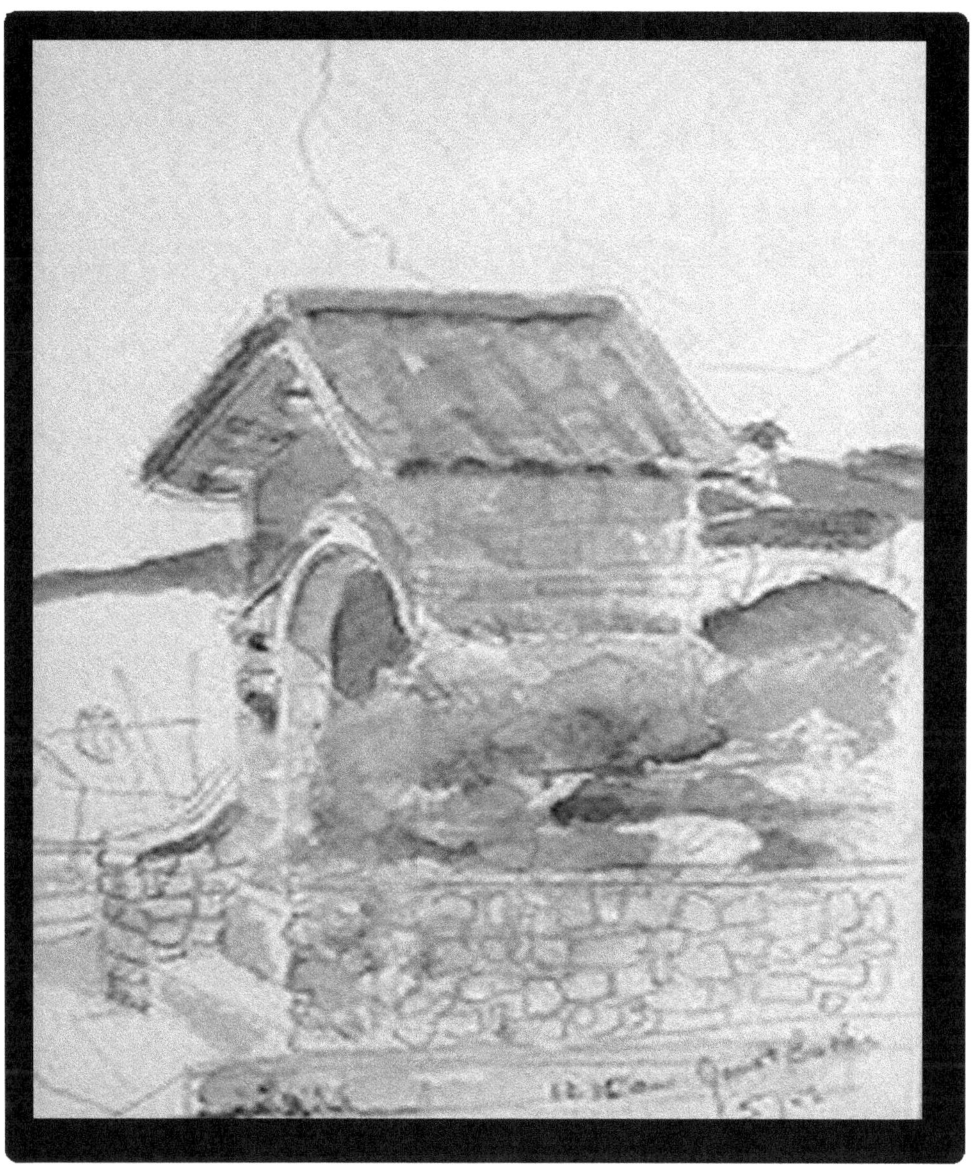

**Street Shrine Perugia, Italy**

**http://fineartamerica.com/featured/street-shrine-perugia-italy-janet-butler.html**

Janet Butler

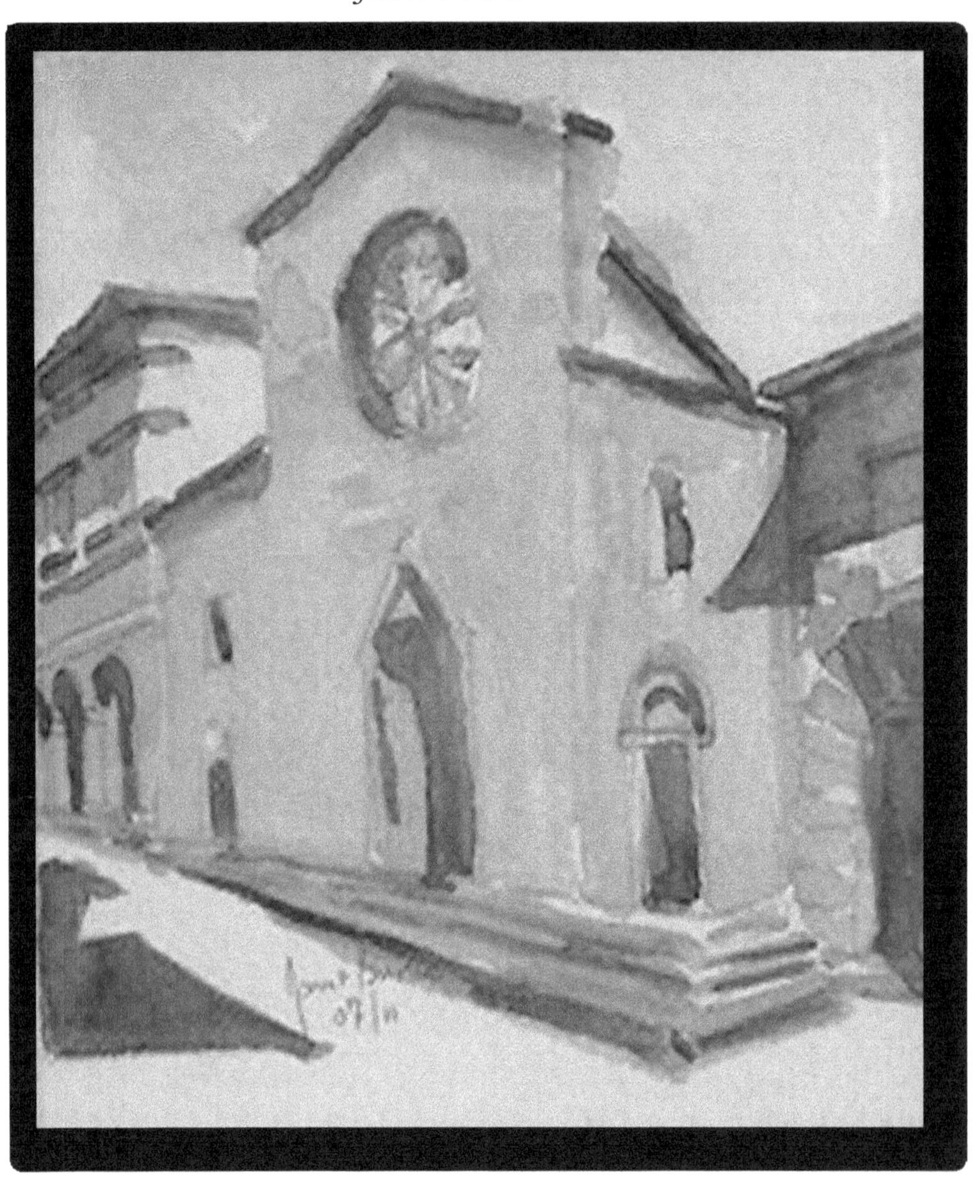

**Church Façade**

**http://fineartamerica.com/featured/church-facade-janet-butler.html**

# Bhopal

AFG.
Indian claim
Line of Actual Control
0 200 400 km
0 200 400 mi
CHINA
Srinagar
Amritsar
PAKISTAN
NEW DELHI
Āgra
Kānpur
NEPAL
Kanchenjunga
BHUTAN
Imphāl
Kāndla
Ahmadābad
Bhopāl
Kolkata (Calcutta)
BANGLADESH
BURMA
Haldia
Mumbai (Bombay)
Nāgpur
DECCAN
Arabian Sea
Hyderābād
Vishākhapatnam
Panaji
Marmagao
Bay of Bengal
Chennai (Madras)
Bangalore
ANDAMAN ISLANDS
Pondicherry
Calicut
Port Blair
Cochin
Madurai
Laccadive Sea
Tuticorin
SRI LANKA
NICOBAR ISLANDS

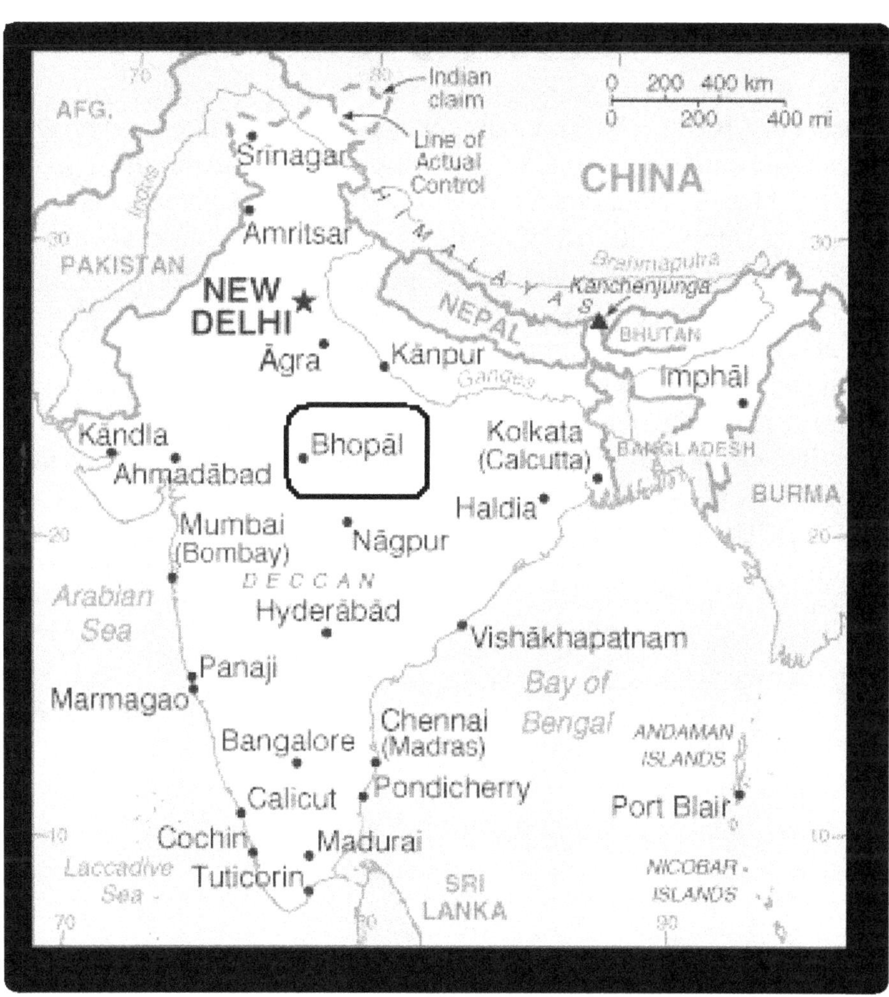

# Elisabeth Khan

Elisabeth Khan is a Belgian-born author and poet who earned an Indology degree from Ghent University. After moving to the USA, she taught Indian Culture at Saginaw Valley State University and French at Detroit Mercy University as well as in various corporate settings. Meanwhile she had several poems and short stories published in Hanging Loose, The Iconoclast, Driftwood, and The MacGuffin. The six years she spent editing and promoting the bilingual publication Gazette van Detroit (started by Belgian immigrants in Detroit in 1914) did not leave her much time for creative writing. She has now returned to her first loves: writing and India. She keeps a blog about her multicultural family, titled Between Three Worlds, on Quora.com and another one, A Writer's Journey On Three Continents, on Wordpress.com. She is currently preparing a poetry chapbook, "The Takht," for publication.

http://betweenthreeworlds.quora.com/

http://elisabethkhan.wordpress.com/

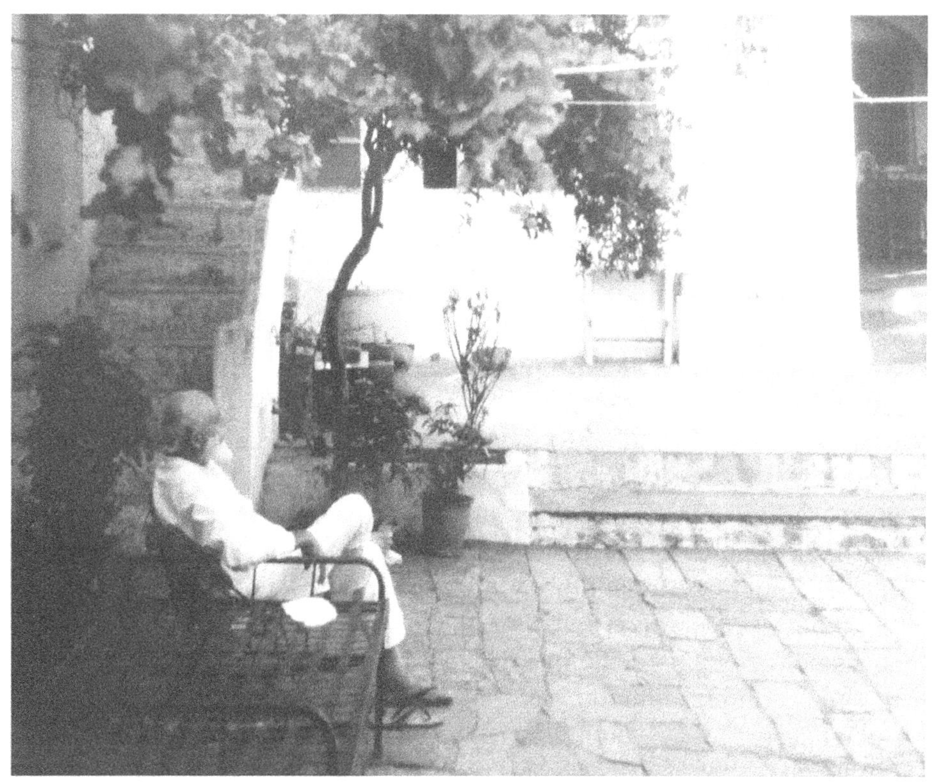

# Bhopal: A Love Story

By:

**Elisabeth Khan**

Elisabeth Khan

The first time I saw–or I should say, experienced–Bhopal was in 1975, and it was love at first sight. I was prejudiced, of course, having become acquainted with a handsome PhD candidate from that town at my university in Belgium. Zafar had made me promise I would visit his city and experience the hospitality of his family and friends.

On our modest student budget my American friend Mary and I had boarded the cheapest flight we could find: Aeroflot–with a compulsory layover at Moscow–and subsequently tramped all over North India for three glorious weeks. We had stood in line for reservations at the Indian Railways' "ladies-only" counter; slept on hard berths in three-tier rail carriages; caught colds from traveling in open-window coaches, soot on our faces and tiny cinders in our eyes on steam engine rides; eaten four-rupee vegetarian *thalis* at roadside shacks; bought cotton clothes made from block-printed bedcovers; slept in no-star hotels where you were supposed to bring your own sheets–of course we had none; drunk the water and gotten sick before becoming immune; savored a tumbler of *lassi* at Udaipur's Lake Palace Hotel, which was all we could afford there; had our sandwiches snatched by sacred monkeys in a Varanasi temple; sat listening blissfully to the *kirtan* [hymns] in Amritsar's Golden Temple, and so much more.

We had been hospitably received by families whose overseas relatives had sent them precious packets of spices through us–like coal to Newcastle, but for a reason: India at the time exported its best products for hard currency–and other small, but much anticipated gifts. In those days of isolationist policies, anything "foreign" was worth its weight in gold.

We had made friends and felt safe even in places where we knew no one, and had been impressed by the innate openness and sweetness of Indian people, their sense of humor, and the way they spontaneously involved us in their sorrows as well as their celebrations. It was early into the State Of Emergency declared by Indira Gandhi, and we were blissfully unaware of its unpleasant aspects. If some people were indignant at the curtailing of their citizens' rights, others appreciated the new work ethic, and everybody was still getting used to the situation. All we noticed was that the trains ran on time and bureaucratic efficiency was greatly increased (it was my second visit to the country) thanks to the Prime Minister's son, Sanjay Gandhi's slogan, "*Kaam zyada, baatein kam* – More work, less talk." Of course, the worst excesses of the notorious "Emergency" were still to come.

Although I had completed the junior year of my Indology studies, my knowledge of Hindi was both insufficient and way too bookish to communicate easily with any passersby. Luckily, we'd always found someone who spoke English to help us out.

And now here we were, dirty and tired, arriving at the railway station of Bhopal, capital of Madhya Pradesh State in Central India. The city at that time was much smaller and quieter than it is today. Few people owned private cars; locals and visitors got around on foot, on bicycles and motorbikes, in scooter rickshaws and horse-pulled tongas. We took a rickshaw. I had a slip of paper with the workplace address of Abdul Rasheed, one of Zafar's friends. It was a garage facing a lake. If Rasheed was surprised, he didn't show it. He was tall, with striking green eyes, and Mary thought him very handsome. Graciously, he took some time off from work to show the way and safely deliver us to the traditional Muslim home where we would be staying. It was late September, and the tail end of the monsoon brought cloudy skies with now and then a light shower, the kind of weather that in India is considered utterly romantic. The perfect weather, hence, to fall in love with a town. Our rickshaw followed Rasheed's motorbike, first on a wide asphalt road, then through narrow, crowded bazaar lanes, before arriving at another, more spaciously urbanized area by another lake. Without our guide, we would probably not have found the house, whose address contained the line, "near Lily Talkies."

The house was built of local stone around a paved courtyard, unto which all but one of the windows gave. The blind wall surrounding it was interrupted only by one heavy wood door and, a little further down, a narrow alley, easily missed, that provided a more discreet, less formal entryway to the inhabitants and their familiars. Rasheed pounded the door with its heavy iron knocker and after what seemed like an eternity, a young man whom I recognized (from photos I had seen) as Zafar's younger brother appeared and let us into a little drawing room that was separated from the courtyard by a curtain. This was as far as our guide could come. He declined the offer of a cup of tea, and after accepting a token glass of water, took his leave. Once the street door was closed and bolted we were ushered into the inner sanctum.

Later I would learn that the room we had first entered, furnished with two sofas, a coffee table and a shelf with sports trophies, was reserved for "outsiders" or formal visitors, in contrast with the rest of the sprawling house and courtyard, which was the private domain of the extended family. Zafar's parents lived there with their children, some of them married, some already parents themselves. It differed from the usual Indian "joint family" arrangement in that not only did the married sons share the compound, but so did the two elder daughters with their husbands and kids. Every nuclear family unit, as well as the unmarried sons, each had their own rooms. Mary and I were put up in Zafar's. The kitchen, bathroom and privies were shared, as was the airy *daalaan*, a cross between a screened porch and a family room.

The courtyard, or *aangan*, was where, weather allowing, most of the day's activities unfolded: early-morning and late-afternoon tea; newspaper reading; visits by assorted relatives; children's games and grownups' gossip; the washing and drying of clothes; the tending of fruit trees (guava, pomegranate), potted plants, and fancy pet pigeons housed in a corner aviary. An hour or two before lunch, one or two ladies of the house would sit on a *takht* [wooden platform] in the courtyard with large trays of rice and lentils, which they would patiently move, a few grains at a time, from one side of the tray to the other, eliminating tiny pebbles and other impurities as they went. They explained to us that the rice and pulses had come from the village, where they had been spread out on the ground to dry. "Would you like to help?" they asked.

Over the next few days, Mary and I shared the life of the family, communicating in a hodgepodge of English and Hindi seasoned with gestures and smiles. The ladies cooked the most delicious dishes for us, dishes that don't appear on the menu of your neighborhood Indian restaurant but are passed down from mother to daughter through the generations.

We admired the way they dressed, in the elegant Bhopali style of a gathered "Turkish" tunic (*turki kurta*) over tight, tapered pants (*tang pajama*). We questioned them about their lives; they were equally curious about ours. One topic, however, was never brought up: the nature of my relationship with Zafar. Arranged marriage was the norm, and the words "boyfriend" and "girlfriend" did not figure in their vocabulary. Whatever attachment he and I had formed could, in their culture, only be a temporary one.

After breakfast each day, two or three of Zafar's friends would turn up and take us out sightseeing in and around Bhopal. They bought us gifts in New Market and helped us navigate the labyrinth of the Peer Gate and Chowk bazaars. They took us to the Lakshmi-Narayan temple with its scenic outlook, and to the imposing pink-sandstone Taj-ul-Masajid [Crown of Mosques], all the while telling us stories about the Nawabs and Begums who had ruled their princely state in its glory days.

But always we came back to the peace and quiet of the house, the warmth of its inhabitants. At more popular destinations in the North, we had sometimes come across unfortunate tourists herded like a flock of sheep in and out of hotels, buses, museums, and monuments. We had considered ourselves part of a different breed: true travelers, choosing where and when to go, how long to stay. Now, however, I felt as if we had crossed another threshold, that of immersion in a culture, seeing not just its external achievements and appurtenances, but living it from the inside.

Before this trip, my professor in Belgium had said to me, "I envy you. It's almost impossible for a man to be admitted into the inner rooms and observe the intimate workings of a traditional Indian home. I'm not talking about the westernized elite in the big cities, but about the middle class, especially in the hinterland." I had not really understood what he meant until now.

Little did I suspect that four years later I would step into this same house as a daughter-in-law; and that, two years after that, I would return to put my first son into his grandmother's arms. Nor could I have anticipated Zafar's frantic attempts to reach his parents from our Belgian home in December 1984, after hearing the news that a toxic gas cloud had escaped from the Union Carbide plant in Bhopal, killing thousands and sickening many more. Fortunately, the family was unharmed. And finally, even in my wildest dreams I could not have imagined that Zafar and I, after many more years and visits, would acquire a house of our own in Bhopal, so that we would be able to enjoy the proximity of the *khaandaan* [clan] and the charms of the city in our retirement.

The Bhopal of today is very different from that of the seventies. The population, less than 500,000 in the early seventies, is now rapidly approaching two million. Despite the tragic events of 1984, the town has grown not only in a demographic and geographical sense, but also in prosperity. The old bazaars are busier than ever, even with the advent of western style malls. New housing developments, new schools and colleges now dot the suburban landscape. The block housing the landmark "Lily Talkies" has been demolished to make room for a "shopping and entertainment complex." This evolution is a mixed blessing. After Zafar's parents passed away, his siblings have taken great liberties with the ancestral home, adding floors to not only accommodate their own growing families, but also to rent out as student digs. This is entirely understandable, an economic necessity even. Yet, every time I behold the old courtyard, now diminished in size and receiving ever less sunlight, I grow nostalgic for the way it was when I first set eyes on it.

# Northern Ireland

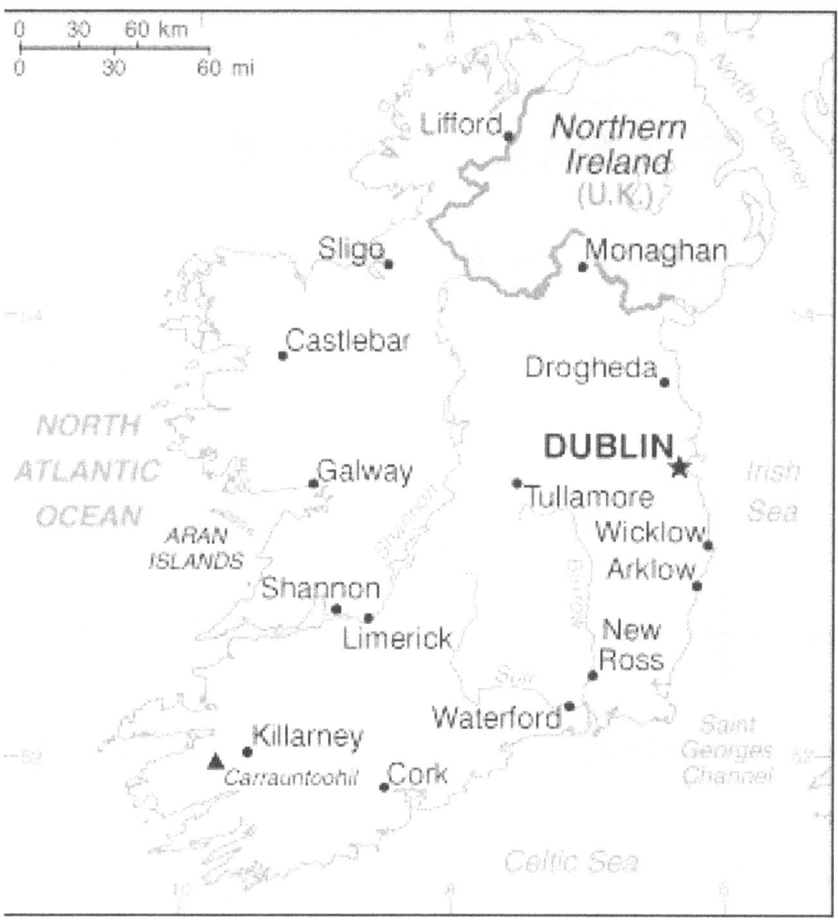

# Emma McKervey

Emma McKervey has been writing poetry since childhood. After spending her 20s working in community arts and childbearing, which distracted her from poetry, she is now studying for a PhD. in Anthropological Studies and ferociously writing poems once again. She lives just outside of Belfast in Northern Ireland.
Examples of her work can be found here:
**Issue Ten - A New Ulster**
https://sites.google.com/site/anewulster/issue-ten
**Gold Dust magazine Issue 26**
**http://issuu.com/golddust/docs/gd26_v16_covers**
She has also had her work included in the University of Ulster Literature anthology Reflexion and in the just published anthology from OWF Press
**Local Poetry**
**http://www.owfpress.com/**

# Celestial Mechanics

In the midst of things did it seem ordinary,
The movement of one moment to the next,
A series of 'and then,....and then,...and then,...'
That seemed normal when you were engrossed?
Or was there a point in Space,
When you looked from the Votok,
And saw the world was blue,
Saw the absence of God,
And you marveled at the path,
From the making of moulds,
To the mechanics of the celestial,
As you made orbit of your home?
Perhaps the accumulation of your time,
Only made its fantastical arc apparent,
In the unexpected moments left to you,
Between the rush of sonic boom and
Your sudden, endless tail-spin
A Mobius fall to Earth.

Emma McKervey

# Drinking Whiskey and Declaiming Yeats to the Wilderness

Two pieces of advice I received before my trek to the Wilds;
1. If a mountain lion is spotted roar, yell, and leap
In an imitation of an inedible predator,
2. If a bear is seen play dead and hope for the best.

This bothered me on my climb, staring off into the aspens and scrub,
Disturbing robins-on-steroids with my high-altitude wheeze.
My companion questioned me on the Wolfhounds he'd never seen as we trekked,
And, as if summoned by the promise of circumstantial awe,
The very beast padded from the dregs of the morning mist.
We were shocked to silence by its mythical presence
Standing to one side reverently to let it pass.

That night I lay in a snow bank and watched a full moon rise
Whilst trout was caught and cooked over the fire.
We drank whiskey and I declaimed Yeats to the Wilderness
And by morning the only predators we'd suffered were the chipmunks
Who'd stolen our breakfast.

# The Frog

I inform the frog that he is in fact
Lucky to be alive. He seems unperturbed
By this information, and frankly
Is lacking in gratitude for my
Having rescued him from the sadistic cat.
He could at least seem mildly embarrassed
About the high pitched screams he emitted
Whilst being batted between clawed paws
But is instead a passive lump
Crouched in the cup of my hands.
I carry him to the stream down the hill,
Usher him safely through a gap in the fence;
He manages an apathetic, lopsided lurch
That drops him in the murk,
And vanishes without a backward glance

# Voodoo

He called me by her name
And I needed to have a shower to rid myself of the
Paunchy bulk of her frame laid over mine
To scrub the familiar bile in my pores
And rinse the metallic taste from my mouth
That comes with guilt and disgust.
Her name is the needle in my voodoo doll
That he keeps in his left pocket,
That he keeps for special occasions, to bring out with a flourish
And watch as he hits his mark.
Then he can fold it away again and walk to the car
Leaving me to my desperate cleansing
As he drives home and pulls from his right pocket
Her own crude and faded likeness.

# Texas

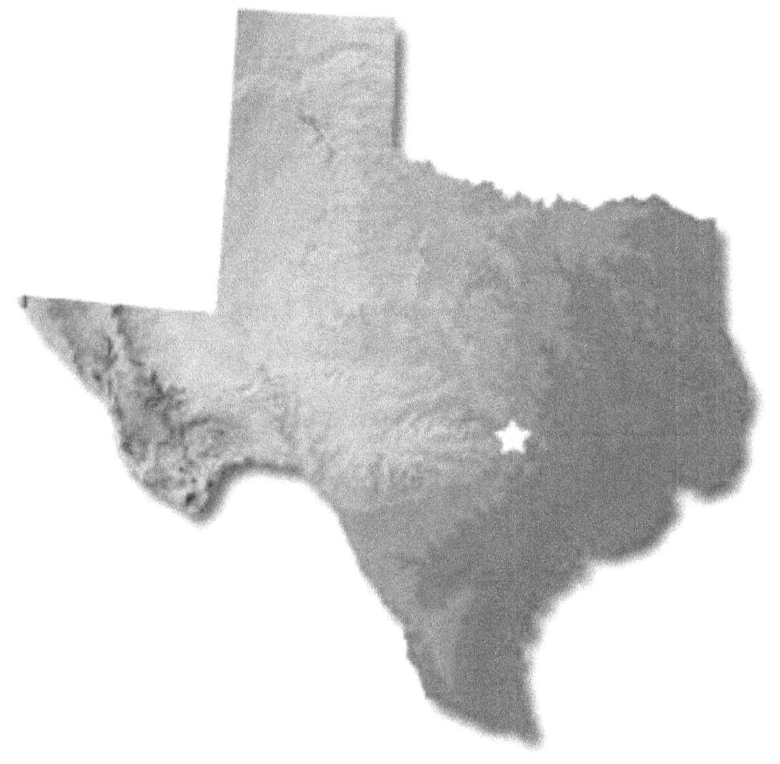

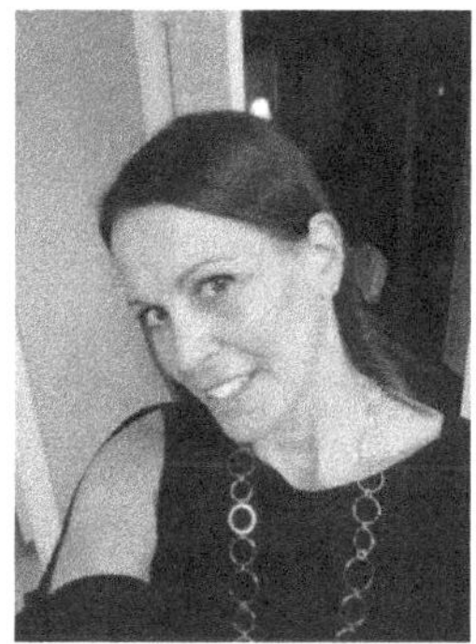

Maria is passionate about writing everything from picture books to adult fiction. She currently pursues writing as a member of Society of Children's Book Writers and Illustrators. Her picture book manuscript, *Step One, Step Two, Step Three and Four*, was a finalist in the National Association of Elementary School Principals Writing Contest. Her middle-grade manuscript novel, *Sushi Kitty*, was nominated for the Joan Lowery Nixon Award, and also became a top five finalist in the National Association of Elementary School Principals Writing Contest. Maria's first short story, "*A Rose By Any Other Name*" placed top five in the Tom Howard/John H. Reid contest with WinningWriters.com. She's a Board Member for the Friends of the Maud Marks Library in Katy, Texas. Maria lives and writes in Katy, Texas with her husband and family. Details about this writer and her current projects can be found at:

**http://www.mariaashworth.com/**

twitter, @maria_ashworth,

**mariaashworth.wordpress.com,**

# 187

By:

## Maria Ashworth

Tanya arrived early and requested a seat by the window overlooking the bay. The hostess obliged her request.

"My husband should be here shortly."

The hostess handed her a menu. "I recommend our Bloody Mary. They're to die for."

Tanya smiled. "I'll take one."

While waiting on her drink, Tanya took in the bistro décor which dripped with shades of red. Assorted pictures of France adorned the walls, putting her in a romantic mood. Once she had her cocktail in hand, she sipped on it while perusing the menu. "Mmm…death by chocolate."

Tanya checked her watch and figured Edward would've rushed over after their earlier conversation. She smiled as she replayed the phone call.

"Hello, Mr. Crick?" Tanya said.

"Yes, speaking."

"I'm Bernice, your wife's secretary."

Edward chuckled on the other end.

"She'd like you to meet her tonight at the new bistro, One, eighty, seven, at six o'clock sharp."

"I'll be there."

Tanya added, "And she said she's not wearing any panties."

"Hmm. . .even better."

Minutes later, the hostess sat a couple beside Tanya. A gray-haired man about sixty, in a sharp blue blazer and crisp jeans pulled the chair out for the svelte blonde who seemed half his age.

Tanya looked cross at the two and took another sip of her drink which suddenly tasted bitter. She eyed the blonde's slender legs and small waist. Tanya sucked in the roll that hung over her waistband and pulled up on her bra straps.

Her curiosity stirred. Tanya appreciated the close proximity of the tables and hoped to hear their story. Her husband's voice permeated in her head, "Eavesdropping again? When will you learn?

The waiter delivered a bottle of some expensive champagne, along with caviar and crackers. He shook out the napkin. "Ms. Thomas," he said laying it across her lap. She smiled, exposing her perfect white teeth. The stout waiter filled the two goblets with the golden bubbly. "Will there be anything else Mr. Baker?"

"No, thank you, Robert."

Tanya bit her lip. Hmm. . . regulars.

Mr. Baker slid his chair toward Ms. Thomas and shared his iPad. Tanya strained to get a glimpse of the screen.

"You ready?" he asked.

The blonde nodded.

"He'll be at Monico's Friday afternoon, correct?"

Ms. Thomas replied, "Yes. It must look like an accident. I don't want people assuming I'm after his insurance policy."

The two chuckled and clanked their glasses together. "To one, eighty, seven. May there be more successful murders to come," Mr. Baker said.

Tanya's eyes widened. She opened her cell and typed in the numbers one, eight, seven. She lost her breath for a second.

The blonde licked her lips. "What about your fee?"

"For you….I'll do it for love." He grabbed her hand then rubbed his thumb over her knuckles.

Tanya hid her gaped mouth behind the menu. Her eyes jumped around the room. Her jaw tightened. Where's the heck Edward?

Mr. Baker said, "I'll make sure there's nothing to trace us to his death."

"Did you get the gun?"

"I purchased a nine millimeter under an alias. It'll be over before he leaves the parking lot," he said.

She laughed like a giddy school-girl. "Perfect. I can't wait to put this behind us and head to the Cayman's on his dollar."

Tanya was startled when Edward leaned down and kissed her on the neck.

"Where the hell have you been?" she snapped.

Edward pulled out his chair. "You sure you're not wearing panties, because they seem to be in a knot."

"Do you know what one eight seven means?"

He set his napkin to his lap. "You use the internet way too much."

Tanya leaned in. "Murder."

Edward shook his head. "Okay, Mrs. Kravitz."

Tanya leaned back. "I hate when you call me that."

"Then stop snooping in other people's business."

Her eyes shifted to the other table. "They're planning a murder," she whispered.

Edward raised an eyebrow. "Do you remember when you accused our ninety-five-year-old neighbor of doing it with the FedEx guy?"

"You have no proof it didn't happen."

"He was her grandson."

Tanya shook her head. "Not buying it."

"And how about the time you thought the third grader down the street was selling drugs?"

"He wanted me to buy some herbs and bath salts."

Edward said, "He was selling them for a school fundraiser."

"All a cover-up," she said waving the butter knife.

He shook his head. "I give up."

They both looked up as the blonde excused herself. Edward watched her walk away. Tanya slapped his shoulder. "Pay attention."

Mr. Baker pulled his cell phone out of his blazer and dialed. "Yeah, I'm here. We're working on it. She'll get it before Friday. You can shoot me if there's a problem." He laughed. "See you tomorrow." He tapped the phone closed as the blonde made her way to the table.

Tanya's eyes widened.

Edward raised his palm. "I don't want to know any more."

Tanya leaned in. "I got to tell her they're planning to kill her instead."

"Stay out of it. Let's eat and get the heck out of here."

Ms. Thomas' hand grazed Mr. Baker's shoulder as she slid into her seat. "So where were we?"

Tanya listened as she picked at the bread nervously while Edward consumed both meals. They paid the check and headed out to the valet.

Tanya stepped in front of him. "We can't just leave. We have to call the police."

Edward gave the ticket to the attendant. "We're getting the car, going home and calling it a night. My nerves are shot. No pun intended."

Tanya looked at him cross. Her eyes strayed. She noticed the advertisement on the wall behind Edward. Murder Mystery Dinner, Friday night. Shut the front door.

As their car pulled up, Edward followed Tanya's eyes. She grabbed him by the arm and hustled him toward the car.

"What's the rush?" She slid in the seat. "I'm not wearing any panties, remember?"

# South Carolina

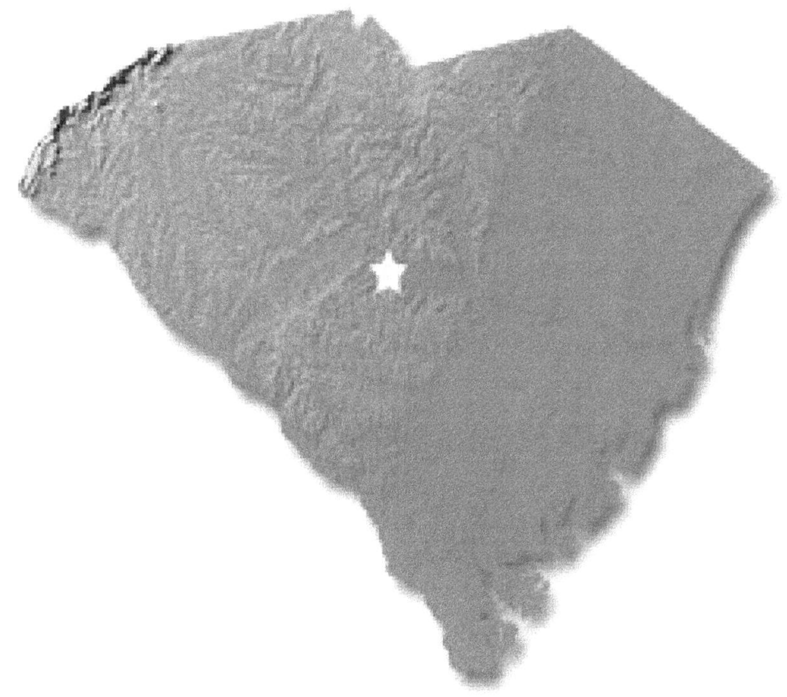

# Stephanie Willimon

Stephanie Willimon, a native of Greenville, SC has been a writer for 26 years. Her first poems were published in the literary magazine, Writer's Inc., through the college she graduated from the University of South Carolina-Upstate. She has been through experiences in her life that at point she didn't write for 8 years. But with a renewed outlook and needed changes in her life, she picked up the pen and paper and came back to her passion.

Links: some of my poems are on my personal FB page (notes section) **m.facebook.com/stephwillimon** and on**writersnet.com**

Stephanie Willimon

# CHEAP SHOT

Those tangible forces of
honeycomb laced words that readily,
yet slowly,
drip from your mouth
with ease are finding it hard
to unlock
this clandestine heart.
My mind has been tangled before
by disclosures of promises,
raptures,
broken peace makers,
and the candy girls walking gently
down the hall
with tiny feet.
Tell me something that these ears
have not heard before
in a chaos of languages!
Can you truly inspire
a desensitized soul?
Is there honesty in your vigilance
in convincing me that
your attributes are noble
but admit where you're ignoble?
Too afraid to walk closer
to your words.
Any moment can rain shovels
from the sky to knock
me out,
senseless!
Only for me to wake up
crying in mute,
while grabbing on to frozen soil,
scrambling to get back my
footing.

Keep them to yourself!
Speaking those words now
would be a cheap shot
to the heavens.

Stephanie Willimon

# LOWCOUNTRY HEATLIGHTNING

Almost out of breath After a long drawn out season Of stagnant breakage And insufficient souls. Now time to sing the Bittersweet song Of goodbyes to a heart Once delinquent and bankrupt. Now welcoming the harvest tide Of joyous polar vortex Rhythm Sweet kisses as fine As a moonlit cup Of salt laced perfection. Blaze across the marsh With a disobedient triumph Of taking grasp of what once Was held captive Until the sincere moment. Brim the trees with touches of autumn As the sun still slices the skin. Fever pitch of the Sweetest magnolia Skips in each word. Can you catch me? Do you even dare? If you do, That will be as magnificent As the low country heat lightning.

# REVERB

Waking up before the dawn breaks in through the window like a dainty thief. Mind and heart overpowered by memories of ones who have ran in and then tiptoed, as if on an icy pond, out of my heart spaces. Overpowering urges, even if it be brief, to place them back into the crevices. I try to keep my heart impregnated so to keep the death of worldly acts from coming back in with the power of 7 times. To revisit these memories induces a mirage of smiles and a collection of prayers to go into the receptacle I treasure with all my self-worth. Songs of the ecstatic New Orleans wake music fill my ears. Is this a God way of telling me to say adios to some of the ones I cherished and held intimately in my arms that were shackled in enslavement of liquid poison? Yes, it must be. For some of those wondrous creatures found me enduring when I allowed myself to be trivial with my spirit. I place these gentiles back out of my heart, beam at them and wish them all the passion life can proposition each of us. I lay my head back down. I let the coolness of the early summer morning penetrate my face. -Stephanie Willimon

# Tennessee

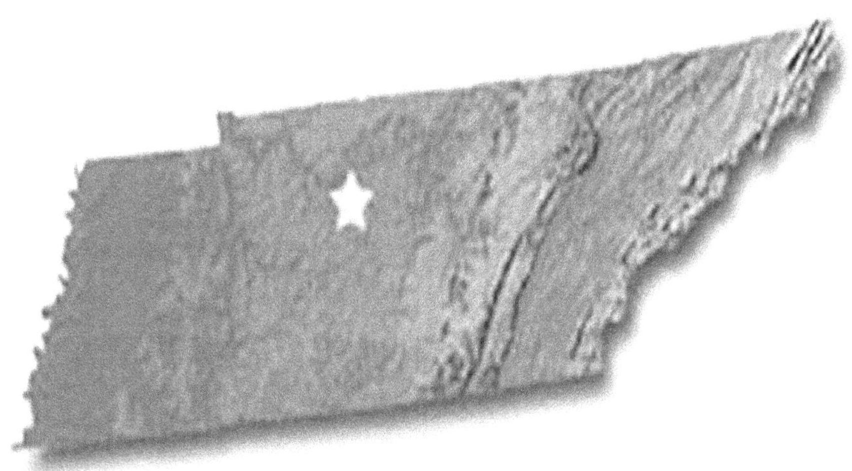

# Stephanie Banks Middleton

Stephanie Banks Middleton, 48, was raised on a fourth generation tobacco farm on the coast of North Carolina. She has been in education for the past 15 years as a Special Education Teacher and school Administrator. She recently moved to Western Tennessee with her new husband Darrell. When she isn't working, she loves to garden, read, and make unique handmade gifts for her business, The Silly Rabbit. Stephanie is a two time Cancer survivor and tries to find something positive in every day. She and Darrell love enjoying the open road on their motorcycles (yes she has her own) and loves taking pictures along the way.

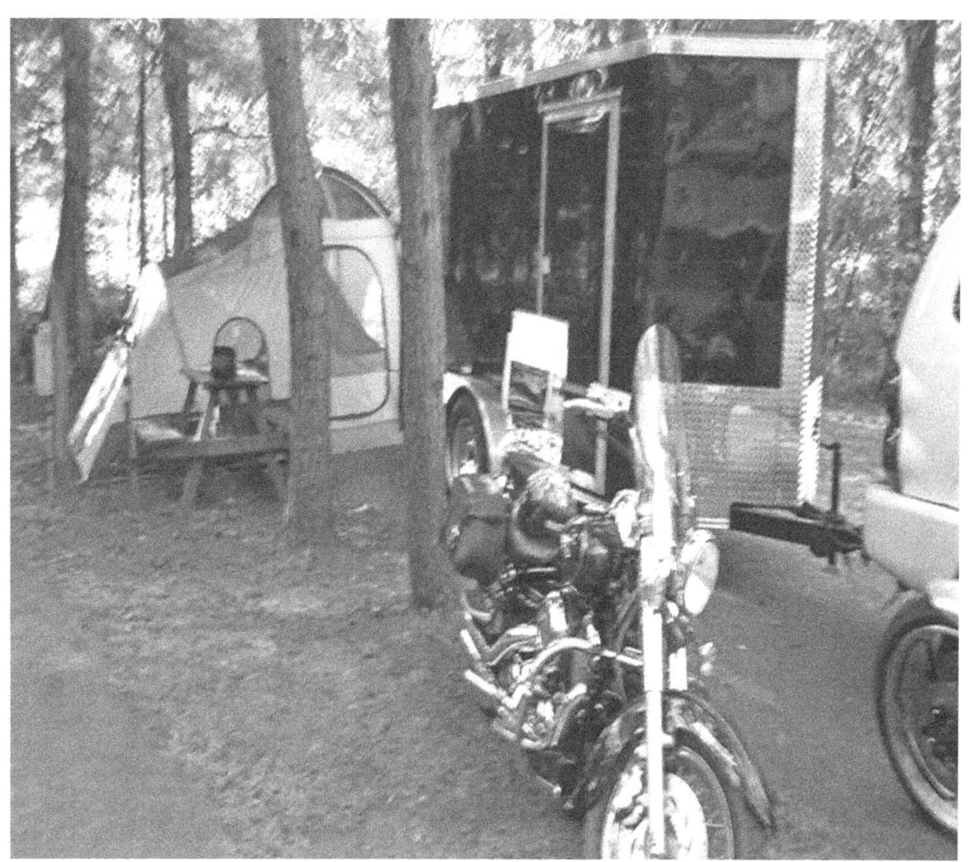

# Dragons, Punkins and Bears...Oh My!!

By:

**Stephanie Banks Middleton**

I was so excited about our trip. My husband (then fiancé) at the time and I had talked about "riding the Tail of the Dragon" for several months and now it was becoming a reality! We made arrangements for a good friend and his girl to join us, unfortunately due to family issues, she was unable to join us, and so the "Three Musketeers" were ready to ride!

I guess I should give a little detail for those of you who are unfortunate, the "non-motorcycle riders", The Tail of the Dragon, is a stretch of mountainous terrain that has 318 curves in 11 miles. It is actually Hwy 129 and considered to be one of the world's foremost motorcycle roads. It begins in North Carolina and snakes it way through end in Tennessee. We live in Western Tennessee so we had a six hour trip (including the time zone change) ahead of us to even begin our adventure.

So Friday morning finally arrived and in the wee hours of the morning our journey began. This was the first time we had not ridden our bikes to our destination of our trips and we were pulling them in our brand new trailer (again one of many first for us). We had been on the road for a few hours when the sun popped his bright head over the tree line, and it was beautiful. This sight reminded me of how blessed we all are and God's beauty is all around us. If you have never seen a sun rise don't wait any longer. I won't waste your time sharing the details and particulars of the rest of our traveling(trust me, it was a lot of out of tune radio sing along, "pit stops" for necessities, bathroom breaks and fast food munchies.

As we went down the last little hill, on what seemed like an endless winding country road (truly Bob's road), we came face to face with the sign, "Dragon Tail this way". Our friend and riding partner, we affectionately call "Kool Aid", spotted a campground sign and since this was our intentions for lodging while on our trip (it was after all Labor Day weekend), we turned in that direction.

Now, I am a country girl, so spending time in the woods; in nature, and with animals close, has always been in my vocabulary. So, to say I was "excited" doesn't do it justice. The other interesting fact was none of us had been "wilderness" camping, by that I mean in- a- tent- with- a- campfire-and a sleeping bag, in the last three years (okay, confession, for me it had been at least 20, but I am the "adult" in the crowd).

We followed the signs toward the campground and the road became increasingly smaller, narrower until it finally turned into a gravel/dirt road (one my grandfather would note as a hog path) and there it is Punkin Center Resort. No sooner did we cross the bridge did I spot the sign "Bear Sanctuary", okay so now, this place has my attention.

We pulled up to the cedar-sided office with adjoining covered outside shelter and we were greeted by two older gentlemen enjoying some liquid refreshments. We all stepped out, stretched, and headed up the steps. Now I should tell you that neither of my riding companions are social butterflies so after I exchanged pleasantries. I asked the man, who I guessed was the owner, how much it would be for a campsite.

He took a long swig (in layman's terms that is a gulp) of his beer and said, "Nice trailer, ya'll gonna sleep in that?"

I shot him a smile and replied "Well now that just depends on how many bears you have here".

Without blinking an eye, he said," Oh, we got em, but only one comes through the camp each night".

Now, at this point I am trying to maintain my composure, but then he continued. He pointed to the dogs lying across the porch, there were a total of four, no pure breeds, just *sooners* or *mutts* as my daddy would call them.

He as serious as he could muster as he states "like clockwork at 3:30 am, he'll make his pass through, but don't worry one of those doggies will sleep at your site, you'll be fine, just don't get up and venture out to the bathroom because the dogs will attack you".

I know I have that deer in headlights look on my face and I can't even make myself respond. Then he breaks out in a big grin and looks at the men in my group and says, "ya'll go ahead and pick you out a sight, get settled in, take in some riding before dark and come back hungry, the pig will be ready around 8 or 9, and we'll just square up in the morning".

So we all retreat back to the truck in silence, but my mind was racing a hundred miles an hour, "just 1? Dogs protect me but attack me? Have I just landed at the edge of a bad B rated movie? I am still stunned.

We choose our site and begin unloading our things. The guys set about putting up our tent, unloading our bikes and I set up out a little home away from home (in other words heeded the sign at the campsite that says don't leave food out, so I'm locking stuff up), but I still can't stop playing the conversation in my head and for me about a hundred and one questions. Are they sure it is just ONE bear? What exactly does it mean" They'll attack you?" and, if I'm in the bathhouse when the bear comes through, do I stay in there? Will someone give me an ALL CLEAR signal? Will one of these fierce protectors come and escort me back to my tent like a bodyguard? (NOTE- the bath house is approximately 50 yards away from our site). So to help me chill out, we decide to go for a quick ride. I must admit it was such a pleasant distraction. The beauty of the mountains, the moving Tennessee River, the brotherhood of fellow riders, it was the peaceful end to a long day of traveling.

Our little entourage returned to our campground just as night began to fall and we built our fire and did the whole cookout thing. This little black dog came up just as I was finishing up the grilling and as we ate, of course we fed her. I chuckled in spite of myself, and this is going to protect me and or attack me tonight if I wander during "bear time".

The forecast for the next day was calling for rain and we wanted to get to our next destination (other parts of the Dragon) before it set in, so we decided to go settle up our bill so we were able to leave early in the morning without disturbing anyone. During the time we had gone out and returned the campground had actually filled up. We walked back up to the "shelter" where several more couples and lone riders had gathered to enjoy a cold one.

The conversations seemed to jump from subject to subject and as most of you know, most of the world's problems are solved in small town gatherings (usually in the back of the local country store). It eventually came back to the topic of our furry friends spread out on the floor among the guests. The same elderly man that had questioned my intentions earlier asked me if I had reconsidered my stay since I was settling up the bill. I again smiled and said no and explained our plans and he surprisingly agreed it was a smart plan. After we listened and laughed (and of course watched a little football on the corner TV) we decided to turn in for the evening. "Remember the rules and you'll be fine," I heard echo behind me as we ascended into the dark walk back to the campsite.

Our friend decided he was going to stay up awhile so he would be able to talk with his lady friend via cell phone. Okay a little history here, they have been known to talk all night on the phone and then meet up just in time to see the sunrise with a cup of coffee on her front porch.

I know what you are thinking, but hey, it is working for them, so to each his own. I just remind him of the warning we had received and told him to be in the tent or in the truck when it got time for our "visitor". One thing we did notice as my husband and I were settling in and getting our night clothes on, one of the larger dogs came to the door of our tent and lay down. I smiled down at him and snuggled under the blanket under the stars. It didn't take long for us to drift off to slumber with the gentle breeze, the grasshopper's songs and the crickets quickly lullabied us to sleep.

Now, I would be fibbing just a little if I said that I didn't wake up wondering what time it was and if I had slept through the main event. And then it hit me, oh no! I had to make a bathroom run! So I fumbled around in the dark and found my boots, grabbed the little mini flashlight and unzipped the door to the tent. The guard dog looked up at me and I whispered, "I know, but man, I gotta go". I headed out toward the facilities and you know how it is, in the dead of the night, pitch black, except for this monstrous light I'm carrying and you hear it.....something is moving behind you. Under my breath I'm praying, "Please let me at least make it to this bathroom and not get eaten by this bear."

Just as I reached the corner of the building, I couldn't stand it anymore and threw a glance over my shoulder and smiled. It was my guard dog! I took care of business (probably a world record time if I had to guess) and headed back to my tent with my shadow right beside me. I got settled back in bed nestled next to my big protective man, whom by the way had not moved a muscle since I left.

I didn't feel him get up but I sure heard the disturbance as the all dogs in the camp came alive almost spontaneously synchronized. It startled me as I sat straight up and I saw my husband standing in front of the window on the opposite end of our tent. His stare was locked and he didn't move a muscle, his breathing was so shallow I strained to see if he was okay, but nothing else on my body moved. The noise level increased so intensely, the best way to describe it was like the rumble and excitement of the NASCAR participants as they approached where you were sitting and passed by you. It only lasted a few minutes but it seemed like an eternity.

As the sound of the dogs got out of range, like a train head down the tracks away from you, my husband returned to bed. "I didn't see him," he reported, "but the dogs sure were raising Cain." My heart was racing as I slid back next to him, I was thinking, okay at least I know what time it is. After a few more tosses and turns and brain outbursts, I fell back asleep.

Daybreak came with the same gentle breeze, the birds were chirping and singing and the sun was warming our faces. Another glorious day and I was alive, not eaten by a bear or attacked by my protector. We scrambled, got dressed and headed out of the tent's door. Who do you think greeted us? Our own personal guard dog! With a quick wag of his tail as if to say, "ALL CLEAR".

The guys start taking the tent down and I heard their chatter about the ruckus (and for those of you that are curious, Kool Aid viewed all of the same sights and sounds we did from the safety of the front seat of the truck. I was loading the truck and trailer and our "guard" quickly moved from the doorway to the two trees in our site about ten feet away and just watched. As we finished up loading the bikes are secured them in the trailer, our personal security got up, stretched as a production worker who just came off third shift, and moved over to the campsite next to us. He took his post right in front of their tent. We just looked at each other and smiled.

So if you decide to travel to eastern Tennessee to ride the Tail of the Dragon, do yourself a favor, bypass the hotels and spend a night or two at the Punkin Center Motorcycle Resort and Campground. You may miss the comfort of room service and amenities, but you can't beat the security.

# Brasil

VEN.
GUY.
SUR.
Fr. Gui. (FR)
COL.
NORTH ATLANTIC OCEAN
Boa Vista
Equator
Pico da Neblina
Belém
São Luís
Manaus
Amazon
Fortaleza
Teresina
Natal
Rio Branco
Recife
Maceió
PERU
Salvador
BRASÍLIA
BOLIVIA
Campo Grande
Belo Horizonte
Tubarao
Vitória
São Paulo
Rio de Janeiro
PARA.
CHILE
Curitiba
Santos
Sepetiba Terminal
SOUTH PACIFIC OCEAN
Porto Alegre
SOUTH ATLANTIC OCEAN
ARGENTINA
URU.
0 300 600 km
0 300 600 mi

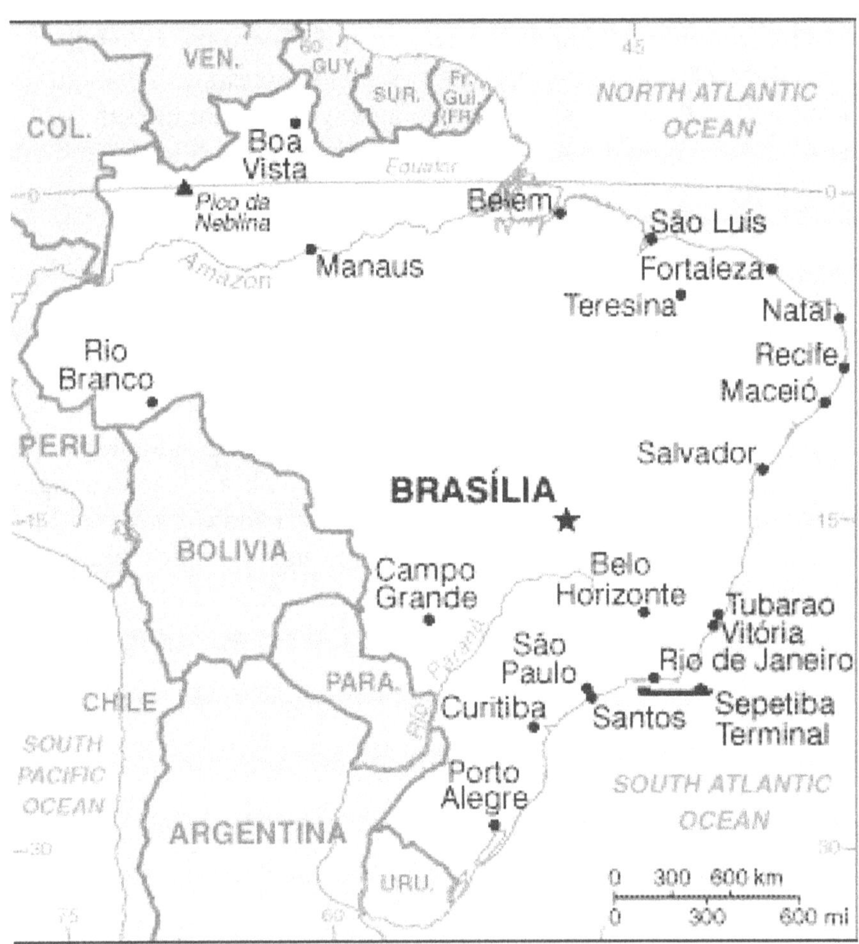

# Dr. Ronaldo Brandão Brochado

Dr. Ronaldo Brandão Brochado is a Physician living in Campos dos Goytacazes, Brasil. He was born in Vitória, ÉS., Brasil. He became a doctor in 1977. He is a general physician. He writes for Country Music News International as a Country Journalist reviewer. He is an avid reader of poetry and is a fan of all genres of music. A great deal of his time outside of practicing medicine is spent trying to bring different kinds of music to South America. His poetry is a mix of styles. He captures a bit of humor in deep stream of conscience thought.

## A FOOL (NOT ON THE HILL...)

I want to be a fool...
If we know about all things....
I became an angry person and boring too...no, no!
Look at to the man that is a fool....
He is smiling ...all the time...
He doesn't know.....
How the dollar is today...the Euro.
What is this? Atômic bomb.
This fool is happy...He believes only what his eyes see.....the moon.
Go to the moon...No it is very far from here....
There's no bus there...in the air....no....
The bus is only on the ground.....
The moon is to gaze at and woo in nights of total peace...
Say the fool: don't be a fool, it all does not exist...my god,
They believe in Santa Claus....
For all of these reasons...
I want to be a fool...
They are happy....

Dr. Ronaldo Brandão Brochado

# True History

In 1964, I was studying in Niterói, a city near Rio de Janeiro...
They were bad times....
Brasil was under the power of military command....
I was in front the sea with a friend named Caio Manlio Serodio...
We ...
Sitting and smoking cigarettes....
Then a car came in racing toward us
        and arrested a man at midday in front of our eyes....
We ran so much ,
With fear ...
Because we witnessed it ....
        and it was very dangerous to us....
Maybe our lives....
Run…
Run....
They arrested a man and till this day
We don't know who he was
If they killed him or not...
I know just one thing ...
We stayed at home for one week....
Filled with all the terror in the world!!!
Bad times...
In these times ...
Students were looked at as bad to these people....
        and they would try to hurt us ...
If we stayed in any one place...
Soon the police would come
We would always have to run...
Now we can look back and see how dangerous it was
The music of this time,
Was of Chico Buarque de Holanda, Gilberto Gil, Caetano Veloso....
They all sang about liberty

# My Mind

My mind works like a windmill....
It goes and comes...bringing times long ago,
Today,
Yesterday,
And all kind of memories,
Really my mind is equal to a horse....
A black horse named Blackstone....
He does all...including flying...
He has wings...
Yes, he...not it...
Because, Blackstone is not a common horse...
These days I go to my father and mothers house
With my friend Blackstone...he eats eggs,
Ten eggs,
Takes apple juice and a little coffee...
He says to me ...give me strength...
Well my father and mother are two wonderful people...
He is 92 years old and my mother 87
I like them both so much...
When I return my father gives me his hands,
And I tell him stay with god....then he says...
Half to you and half to me!
And I think how mysterious life is...
My father maybe does not recognize us...
But this time...I go home happy...
My horse Blackstone and I....
Blackstone helps me do music reviews....
He and his wife are musicians...
They studied in Paris...
His wife is a sweet lady....what Black?
Yes, I'm writing to Jeremy Frost...
Yes he does reviews for CMNI also...
Jeremy, Blackstone sends greetings to you...yes,
I understood what he said....I tell you,

He has personality....and knows all about music...harmony, vocals, drums....when you need....
Great hug to our crazy people....
Life is good, and dreams are wonderfullllll!

# Brasil

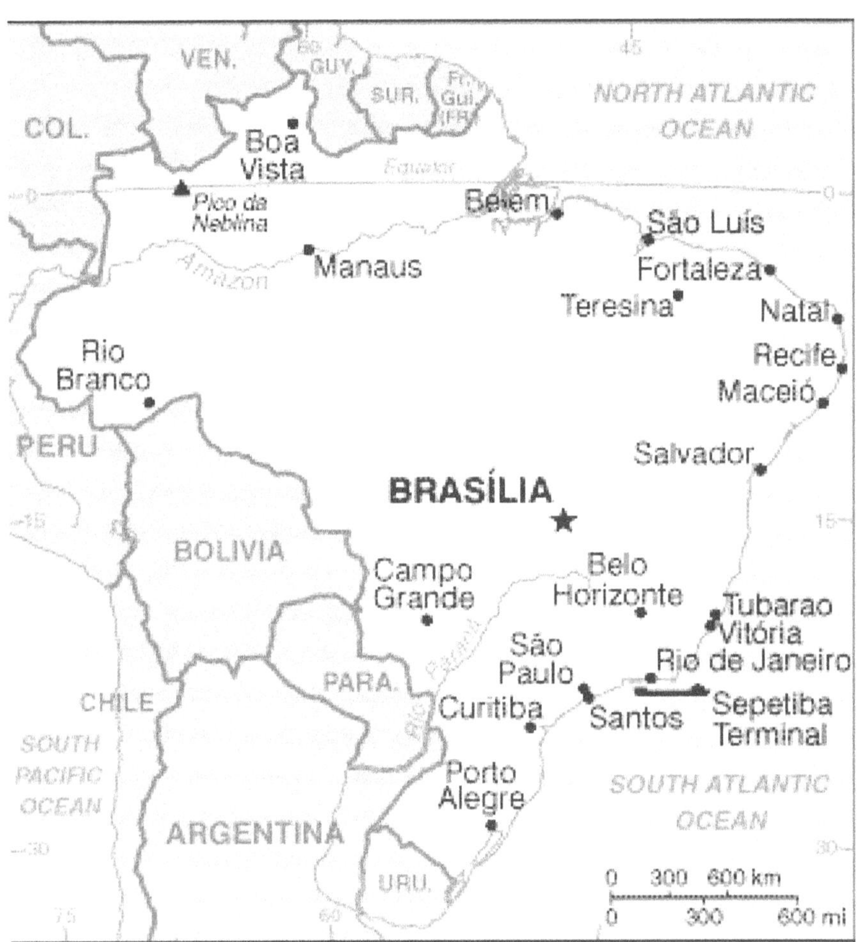

# Mauro Leite Teixeira

Mauro Leite was born in Aymores E.S. He Lives in Vitória E.S. Brasil. He has a great love for poetry and the arts in general. He focuses a lot of attention on the daily life in Brasil. The politics and thoughts of life are reflected in his poetry. He is an engineer by profession, but has held numerous titles throughout the years. Director General, Secretary of Transportation, superintendent, vice president and then president of a community service organization. His poetry has been left in Portuguese here because it may lose its feel in translation.

# FETICHE

No fim da tarde
Sem fazer alarde,
Toda faceira,
Foi pra cidade.
Entrou no Shopping Center
Pensando...
Comprar a felicidade.

# DESAFIOS

Mundo danado de misturado!
Difícil de decifrar,
Como vou me convencer?
Pra poder me situar?
Falar no celular...
O sertão vai virar mar...
Tudo é arisco e vai mudar
Vou ler, pra entender.

# MOVIMENTO

"O sol é novo a cada dia"
A estrela da manhã
O amanhecer anuncia.
O astro-rei navega no firmamento...
O entardecer...
Traz melancolia.
Sentir o correr do tempo
Tem serventia.

# A Hedgerow of Book Stacks

**by: Michael Christopher Markman**

This is how I picture most reviewers' homes. Their walls are lined with wall to wall books, for those books next on their list to review. They get books in the mail and they stack them wherever they can in the hopes they'll remember where it went when the time comes.

This said I tried to pick books from several genres that I thought I might enjoy. The reason being, I know if I didn't enjoy it... I wouldn't finish it, and that still happens once in a blue moon... Also, if I enjoy it, there is at least a better chance my audience will find something in it that will be entertaining, or education. However, I cannot guarantee that because I liked a book... you will like it, but... by reading my commentary I am hopeful that you will be able to gauge for yourself whether or not the book will be of interest to you.

# "The Spells"

**By: Gary L. Morton**
**A Frightlibrary.org book.** 2014.

I gotta admit when I started reading this book there were a couple things that came across to me as uber hokey, and one of them was the "evil" heat spells that are referred to in the book's title.
The book is set in a future version of Toronto, with high security high rises, robots, near zombie drug addict gang members, an underground prison, and a super villain known as "the Doctor." Which means, I can't claim that the hokey ever goes away entirely, but I didn't care. It was a fun read.

If I were to try and classify the book I'd say it felt like it was one third comic book, one third detective novel, and one third James Bond novel. The addict gangsters known as Blues made me think of the recent Crocodile epidemic in Russia. The Doctor felt like he was part comic book character, part Bond-esque Villain. Nevertheless, the author kept the action consistent, and the pace always on the move. This book was an enjoyable read.

# "Smoking Springs"

**By: Robert C Mowry**

**Tru-Con Publishing**. 2012.

This book is a Western. It is set toward the end of the Civil War, and it explores the life of two soldiers, and their companion a slave... as well as the various people they meet upon the trail. The wounded soldier, Judah Ward, struggles to regain his health after being severely injured in battle. As with most people during this time, that battle is more with infection than anything else. He also struggles with a conservative upbringing by a Hellfire and Brimstone style preacher... something that could harden even compassionate hearts against religion.

As a fan of the old Louie Lamoure style westerns. This book has a genuine feel to it, as the characters change and grow as individuals. I highly recommend it.

# "Cosmic Rift"

**By: J.P. Osterman**

J.P. Osterman. 2014.

If you like Science Fiction, space travel, and books that explore and attempt to extrapolate how technology will grow and develop in the years to come...

The main focus of the book is about space exploration as the ships commander and co commander go in search of other habitable planets. I really, really liked some of the concepts the author explored in regards to computers with a direct to human interface and the problems that might result.

While I do feel that the author wrapped things up... "a little too neatly toward the end". I nevertheless enjoyed this book a great deal. I liked the author's ideas. The book obviously took a great deal of thought, and it felt like a great deal of research to create a sense of realism that has fallen out of favor with some of the more modern science fiction. This author is going to be one of the future heavy hitters...

Just you watch, and see....

# "The Harem Games"

## By: **Jorge Carreras Jr.**

If I don't like the way a story begins. I still try to give book every chance I can when reading them... in the hopes I will find some redeeming quality. This said I could not get myself to finish this book. The title of course made me think, this guy is trying to make money off "the Hunger Games" franchise. Good luck, buddy. Which, it was post apocalyptic, with a hint of the comic "Y the last man"'s plague that wipe out all the men on Earth...

From there it went to the surviving descendants of a lone immortal human, and the competitions held between harems each year. The men, are all stereotyped, except our hero the hermaphrodite, who happens to be the ultimate lover, and ultimately consider of women's needs, and able to commune with animals and velociraptors; and find their gentler more nurturing side.... oh, and did I mention that they all have super powers...

Yeah, and that was as far as I got... If you want to try it out. More power to you, but... not my cup of brine.

# "Monsters All the Way Down"

## By: Ryan Mcswain

### Pithos Publishing. 2014.

I have to admit this wasn't the book I had expected... Which is always a delight. It had the feel of conspiracy theories and spy novels to start, and then grew into something else.

While there was a slight matter of... what I call the "hokey factor" which occurs with some science fiction books. This said, I think the author did a good job in how it played out. The action was good, the bad guys weren't just all bad... and the author set about to create a world that had depth.

# "Exo"

## By: Stephen Gould

### A Tor Book. 2014.

This is a book by the author of Jumper. What I like best about this book is that the author's characters continue to grow and attempt to explore their abilities, looking for new ways to push past the boundaries set by those who came before them, and their own limits.

I like that.

I like when people explore and test the boundaries of their environment in fiction, almost as much as I do in real life. It is the kind of thing I do when day dreaming, and that is another reason I think it makes for great fiction. It is the kind of narrative you yourself might do, if you discovered you had the power to teleport.

While I do think there was less action than I might have liked... The author did make up for it by taking us through a brainstorming session on how he would explore this ability.

**The "CoffeeShop Blues" is an international literary journal. It showcases artists from around the world, poets from all the corners of the globe, and writers who have stories to tell. It is published by Coereopsis Publications LLC, out of Florida. We are a small group of artists that put these together at least annually. We are constantly open to read submissions but until our next issue is decided upon, cannot give an acceptance. You can check us out at our webpage** www.Coreopsis.gs **or email us at Coreopsispress@gmail.com**

www.ingramcontent.com/pod-product-compliance
Lightning Source LLC
LaVergne TN
LVHW020631100826
845148LV00012B/2140

* 9 7 8 0 9 7 6 3 0 2 9 5 7 *